# Venezuela

## A DEMOCRACY

*Caracas, capital of Venezuela.*

# HENRY J. ALLEN

# Venezuela

## A DEMOCRACY

NEW YORK

Doubleday, Doran & Co., Inc.

1940

# *Foreword*

---

SOMETHING LIKE FOUR YEARS AGO I filed a copy of the map of Venezuela for future reference.

Current dispatches had carried the story that this South American nation had just buried a dictator, General Juan Vincente Gómez, who had died a natural death, and that it had during the same week become a republic.

This I knew was important, if true.

Shortly after he entered upon the duties of his office, the new President announced that the government would initiate an intensive social-service, welfare and economic program. The 1938 Congress, a few months later, approved a budget of 1,210,140,000 bolivars to be expended over a period of three years in the furtherance of these objectives.

Three cogent things impressed me about this program:

First, a government was setting out to improve the

v

status of its people by improving their health, the individual's most precious possession; to increase their opportunities for education, the individual's best guaranty of self-dependence and economic opportunity, in an effort to place both the people and the nation on a secure, self-supporting basis.

Second, the government announced its intention to spend on this program about $400,000,000 in three years, a tidy sum for a nation of less than 4,000,000 people to spend on a social program.

Third, the present administration in Venezuela was able to embark upon this program because of the fine fiscal condition of the government. It had inherited not only a debt-free, interest-free government, but even more important, it had inherited also a cash balance of 120,000,000 bolivars from the previous administration and substantial current revenues. Since the cash balance and current revenues could not together provide adequate funds to pay for the program, the balance was to be provided by a foreign loan which has not yet materialized.

Now nearly two years of this spending program had gone. Official sources of information indicated that this substantial, comprehensive plan was making progress in a land which, when the program was launched, had a balanced budget, no national debt, a surplus in the treasury, no unemployment, no relief rolls and very few direct taxes.

It seemed Venezuela had, in fact, everything that

European dictators have been subduing their neighbors to obtain. So why shouldn't she have a republic, since she could afford it?

I came to Venezuela as men travel to a land of fables.

Near the end of the Five Year Plan in Russia, I had gone to the Soviet Union to see the miracles under the overadvertised procession of events, and came home holding joint debate with everyone who had read the Russian propaganda.

Therefore, I was prepared to be disappointed in the accomplishments of the Venezuelan program.

But I was not prepared to discover that the plan, which had been officially operating less than two years, was really two years ahead of the time in respect to important parts of the social improvements contemplated in the program.

There had been already large expenditures for sanitation, hospitals, education, agriculture and port improvements.

The people were astonished by the new things they were witnessing.

The streets of Caracas, the capital of Venezuela, were ripped wide open for the installation of new water works. Impressive hospitals either had been finished or were being built in Caracas and in cities elsewhere in the Republic.

New ministries buildings already had been finished, paid for and occupied. The land was full of foreign experts checking up the projects. Highway and railway engineers, sanitation experts, water-works experts and other engineers who were conducting miscellaneous surveys of the nation's agricultural and mineral possibilities, and the architectural experts who were planning new cities, all served to make me realize that this Venezuelan program—more spiritual and political than economic—is, nevertheless, the most realistic program ever undertaken in South America.

By the time I had spent some weeks in looking at what they were building, I realized there is little comparison between the meanings of the word "plan" as uttered by President Lopez Contreras of Venezuela and by the prophets who have been planning in other parts of the world.

For example, in the program proposed by the President of Venezuela there was an elaborate set-up for education. It was to start during the biennium 1938–39. Amongst the first evidences I saw of its operation, however, was a new building for the Minister of Public Education, already finished and paid for—a chaste and beautiful structure from which there emanated an educational movement which already had expressed itself in hundreds of new schools, thousands of new pupils, and millions of bolivars expended for teachers' salaries and school equipment.

It is too soon, of course, to appraise the product of the schools. Doubtless Venezuela is making and will continue to make, in the conduct of her educational program, something of the mistake we made in the

Philippine Islands, when we forced education upon members of the population not yet properly prepared to benefit by it.

When educational training makes men and women of limited intelligence and capacities dissatisfied with their old ways of living and working without equipping them to render either more useful or better-paid services, then it is certain to contribute to the discontent and inactivity of a people. We have found, on the other hand, that if education can be adjusted to the needs and capacities of the people, it thereby enables them better to create wealth in the form of services or goods for the use of others by sale or exchange, and it can and does add greatly to the national contentment and wealth. When education does this for the people of a nation, then that nation prospers.

The speed and effectiveness with which these earnest Venezuelans got their program under way make one believe that they deliberately launched it ahead of schedule.

Upon arrival in Caracas, the first man I asked about business startled me by saying, "It is booming." I hadn't heard that reverberating word uttered in reference to business for ten years.

When I left New York six days before, I had wired for my accommodations in Caracas because my friends told me that hotel rooms were hard to find. The Majestic management had reserved the rooms on the day they received my message, held them for me, and charged me room rent for the six days I was traveling to reach the land!

When I showed a disposition to be annoyed at the manner in which they had taken time by the forelock, they assured me that after all I was lucky. They could have leased those rooms the day they received my telegram and every day since. I had told them I must have the accommodations, and they took no chances. Otherwise I might have been obliged to wait six days after my arrival for the rooms. Thus they comforted me.

Instances of this kind occur only in lands where some kind of boom is going on. The high cost of living, the increasing demand for labor, coupled with top wages, make it a country which is plunging ahead with income relatively high and expenditures more so; and probably with no greater results in popular profits than generally occur whenever and wherever profits are being gained from an industry whose expenditures are out of proportion to the normal economy.

After all, the astounding thing about Venezuela is not in its economic good health. Any nation receiving more than a third of its income from petroleum production that runs to 600,000 barrels a day, supplemented by its other revenues, and with no debt, might have a slightly apoplectic tendency in its economic system. Even individuals who strike oil find that the discovery afflicts their pocket nerves.

But in Venezuela the point is in the character of the temptation that now excites its spending impulses.

Probably in the long history of the world no nation has achieved so sudden a passion for social service and public welfare as that which now manifests itself in Venezuela. Certainly no nation in the world ever before launched a program of this nature when so much information about it had only recently been made available. History may call it providential that this passion coincides not only with the need of a people but with revenues or credit at hand for carrying out such a program.

When your mental process seeks a comparison of Venezuela with anything else that has happened in Latin America, your mind clicks on the late President Diaz of Mexico. He was about the same sort of dictator as was Gómez. During most of their lives they were contemporaries. Each benefited his country industrially by fair and friendly dealing with foreign capital. When Diaz faded out of the picture in Mexico, his enemies came into power and chaos arrived which remains unto this day.

No marked change of administration personnel took place after the death of Gómez. Several members of his official family remained in power, and except for a brief flare-up and a little bloodletting, there was no disorder. The great change was one of spiritual direction which now seeks to transform the social order in the name of a constitutional democracy.

I am not going to write about the horrors of Venezuela. They have had sufficient attention. That malaria, syphilis, tuberculosis and parasite diseases have thrived in a country of poor sanitation, limited hospitalization and tropical encouragement to all forms of malady, cannot be denied. Nor is there any disposition on my part to gainsay that the masses have been slowed down by circumstances existing in all tropical countries where primitive conditions have long existed in agriculture and industry.

Instead I am going to write of the fresh promise that has come to this land through the happy union of a sufficiency of revenues or credit and the anxieties of its leaders to accomplish a genuine humanitarian program. If they are truly successful with this program—and they should be if the government continues to encourage investment by private capital and does not let its enthusiasm lead it into spending more than it can afford—they will do more than care for the sick and needy and bring education to all. Fundamentally they will create and inspire new individual strength, independence, initiative and productiveness and thereby maintain economic sufficiency.

Venezuela has much to do. Her task is not alone the perfection of her pattern of government but the sure advancement of her people. She has made a brave start upon problems by first making their bodies and minds well and strong. The effective completion of this program will require generations. Something will depend upon the persistency of a people not heretofore noted for this quality.

This book is going to deal with her problems and the way in which she is attacking them. To verify facts, I have traveled to all parts of Venezuela, even reaching remote spots on the Grand Savannah, the borders of Colombia in the Amazonian region, Brazil and British Guiana on the south and east. The visit included trips to the gold mines, the fisheries, the diamond fields, the iron-ore deposits, the vast plains of potentially rich agricultural lands, and the noble rivers which make both water and land transportation possible. I have visited the oil fields, of course, but I have spent much time upon the study of other natural resources, the development of which must insure the distant future of this favored land.

Nothing needs to be done by Venezuela to improve the oil industry. The last word in science is used in the proper development of these great resources, the unexpected limits of which continue to enlarge under modern exploration. The relations between the government and the petroleum interests are cordial and cooperative. The continuance of such relations will encourage the investment of more and more foreign capital in the exploration and production of oil.

But an effort is now being made to build up the other possibilities of the country to match the petroleum development. As they work at this task, these Venezuelans should grow in strength, efficiency, productiveness, and desire to render useful service to society.

For the present Venezuelan officials have planned with fine intelligence and splendid purpose; they are operating with ability and integrity.

I have lived most of my life in active areas of the mid-continent oil fields and have seen unexpected, sudden and great wealth come to countless farmers on whose land oil had been discovered. Not more than a handful of such men planned and carried out the spending of their new wealth with ability, intelligence and vision. If it is difficult for individuals, it is doubly hard for government to spend new wealth ably, intelligently and with vision.

While they have conceived greatly and have worked with rare ability and high integrity, their greatest job lies ahead of them—that of knowing just when to put the brakes on spending. History has proved over and over again that the spiritual lives of a people can be destroyed by too great or too prolonged government spending; that that government which opens opportunities for its citizens, which stimulates their desire for economic independence and encourages their initiative is the one which breeds a great people. A bitter truth which free-spending nations have learned is that assistance designed to create self-supporting men and women is separated only by a hairline boundary from the assistance which creates dependent men and women.

And history has proved over and over again that once the people of a nation get too dependent upon government pap it is almost impossible to wean them. Today's

Venezuelan officials have blazed many new and splendid trails—perhaps they can confine government spending to the safety point before the dread disease of spiritual and intellectual and physical stagnation manifests itself.

The task which now drives these fortunate leaders has possessed their imagination. This book will seek to reveal their present very remarkable progress, their future prospects and problems.

# Contents

xvii

# Illustrations

---

# Venezuela
## A DEMOCRACY

# CHAPTER I

## *A First and Last Chance*

---

BOUND FOR VENEZUELA on a Grace liner from New York you pause a part of the fourth day at Willemstad on the Dutch island of Curaçao. It is the literal last chance to buy merchandise before you reach the high-tariff zone of Venezuela.

Free trade allures the passengers to go ashore and look upon the well-stocked stores. Perfumes from Paris, tobaccos from the choicest fields of the Dutch East Indies, rare merchandise from all over the glamorous protected world are displayed here, inviting the traveler to load up at the last free port he will find on his journey through the Caribbean.

Curaçao is only a little dot of land in the Caribbean, but it has always been potent as a trading center. In its early history it attracted the pirates of the Spanish Main, who always found there something worth carrying away. Three of the most indomitable of these sea robbers, Balthami Carion, Juan Antonio (Dios de la

Robbia) and D'Estrades ended their lurid careers upon the gallows of this island they had so often plundered.

In 1643 the Parliament of Holland appointed Peter Stuyvesant to unite the colonies of Curaçao and New Netherlands, and on July 28, 1646, he became governor of this new union with headquarters at New Amsterdam, now New York. From that time to the close of the American Revolution, over a hundred years after, Curaçao vied with Boston, New York and Philadelphia as a trading center. A large part of its early commerce was the slave trade. It resulted in an admixture of Negro blood in the native population of Curaçao. Slavery was abolished in 1816.

The island has a language of its own for the native population. The various nationalities which have guided its destiny have resulted in a polyglot known as "Papiamento" which has no grammatical rules but is composed of words from the Spanish, French, Dutch and English vocabularies.

The Dutch Shell now operates a main refinery at Willemstad, where it processes a part of the Venezuelan oil produced only a night's ride away. This refining of the Venezuelan export makes a busy shipping center here.

Willemstad presents a picture as typically Dutch as Holland without windmills. It has a population of some sixteen thousand, mostly Indian and Dutch mestizos. The island of Curaçao has altogether something over thirty-five thousand people. Cleanliness and order characterize it, as in every Dutch colony I have ever seen. Its houses contain many suggestions of Dutch architecture. Its free port makes it a shopping Mecca for tourists. As the passengers stream back to the boat they are loaded down with packages, talking happily about the bargains you get in a land that has no tariff.

I stood for a long time that night gossiping with a fellow traveler and observing the native labor busy on the wharf with the cargo. Said the traveler, "It now takes three stevedores to do what one accomplished a few years ago."

Looking at the wharf I saw that practically every package had available six men to handle it and one man to boss the operation. If the package called for the use of only one man, he passed it on until the six men had taken some part in transferring it.

My companion explained that these men once got seven cents an hour for a ten-hour day, now they get thirty cents an hour for an eight-hour day.

"We multiplied their wages four times and lightened their load six times," he said.

I asked him what effect the larger wage had produced on the workers.

"They all wear shoes," he replied. "This marks the most rapid advance in the living scale."

As I stood watching them dig American automobiles and canned goods out of the hold of the ship, I heard two Standard Oil men, Venezuela bound, talking about the tempo of the dock labor, which they also were

watching. One was an old-time staff man in Venezuela;
the other apparently was a newcomer. The newcomer
complained about the obvious shirking of the stevedores, who had a sort of WPA speed, slightly stepped
up.

The man experienced in South American ways said
this, which was to stay with me during my long days in
Venezuela: "It's a trying climate in which to work—
it doesn't make for either speed or strength. We become
accustomed to delay. We do not complain that these
men do their work slowly. We are satisfied that they do
it willingly."

They didn't get all the American cargo unloaded
until very late. A great crowd of Willemstad visitors
were in the bar veranda, the dining room, deck parades
and swimming pool. They were all over the ship, keeping every waiter and bartender busy. The orchestra
played and the dance continued unabated as the stevedores labored with the cargo.

I was told that this is a performance which goes on
once every week when the Grace liner waits here to
unload its cargo. The occasion has become an Old
Home night with Willemstaders.

I said sleepily to the steward, "This must be a very
profitable night for the ship."

"Too many of them are complimentary," said he.
"Our best local customers come down and bring the
town's dignitaries, and we stand the treat."

So I said "Good night," and he said, "It will be hot
when you get up in the morning at La Guaira."

## CHAPTER II

# *The Ancient Highway*

---

LA GUAIRA, where the tourist hesitates briefly before ascending into Venezuela proper, has a brilliant harbor full of sapphire and emerald tints. A towering Andean range now and then casts waving shadows over it.

The harbor is to be improved and enlarged. Thirty million bolivars—$10,000,000—have been set aside for this purpose.

I learned this while waiting to answer questions about my family history, my past and my hopes of the immediate future, for the discussion of which the passport regulations contain provisions.

Friends told me of the 250,000-bolivar hospital, then building, the new sanitary unit, the new sea colony for all the school children of the federal district, and the new La Guaira water works, evidence of which could be seen in the ripped-up streets.

So by the time I was finally stamped and approved by the customs and immigration officers, I knew that the sprawling town of La Guaira, jammed between the Andes mountains and the Caribbean, was being made over.

For some time I had been remembering what the ship's steward told me the night before about the temperature at La Guaira. My friends assured me I would forget it as soon as we started for Caracas.

In due time we set out upon the ancient highway of Venezuela, which takes you first upon a mountain adventure of curves that corkscrew several thousand feet into the air and then bring you down into a valley where the capital city of Caracas nestles three thousand feet above sea level.

The elevation makes the temperature agreeable. It felt like the resort weather of Colorado Springs during the summer.

The old road was a whirligig. It kept you painfully alert because you were never looking at the same view any length of time. Frequently, as the car whirled around a mountain curve above a monstrous declivity, you swallowed your epiglottis out of sheer terror.

At one place along the serpentine way, passengers are shocked by a monumental sign by the roadside. Built of cement to suggest a large tombstone, some twenty feet in height, it is meant as a warning to drivers. A copper plate embedded in the face of the marker says in Spanish, "Slowly One Goes Far."

Perched on the broad top of the structure is a wrecked automobile, reclaimed apparently from a neighborhood

accident. Its bent fenders and crushed body give poignant realism to the admonition. Broken guard rails at
frequent places along the road should inspire added
respect for the advice to go slowly. As I reacted to the
swirl of traffic around these curves, I felt that the warning was being taken too lightly by the present drivers.

This road connects with the Trans-Andean highway
which is the longest and best-known in Venezuela. It
proceeds from Caracas westward for eight hundred
miles, across mountains sixteen thousand feet high, over
valleys, past seaports, jungles, pastures and farms. Along
its sinuous way you enjoy a panorama of Venezuela's
tropical kingdom, including the birds of the air, the
beasts of the forest, and the flowers in the most beautiful
exhibition of nature's extravagance I have ever seen.

Finally the road crosses the Táchira River near the
Colombian border on a steel bridge named "Bolívar,"
by which the ancient way passes into Colombia, proceeding to Bogotá, the Colombian capital. The highway,
which is called the Trans-Andean, is not paved after
you reach Puerto Cabello, except for an eight-mile
stretch near San Cristóbal which is asphalted.

Tourists from the ships take this road from La
Guaira and traverse it 130 miles through Caracas, Maracay, Valencia, and down to Puerto Cabello, where
the ship they left two days before at La Guaira waits
for them in a modern dock of the most rapidly growing
Venezuelan port.

Four hundred years of Venezuelan history have trav-

eled over this road. When it was a rude mountain by-
path, the clanking Conquistadors used it. Simón Bolívar
made his way over these passes and through these valleys when he came home from Paris 125 years ago,
bearing to his beloved Latin America his interpretation
of the French Revolution.

Gómez and his followers, from their Andean fastnesses in far western Venezuela, traversed it forty years
ago when they came to make secure Castro's fight for
the "Restoration," as he called his revolution. It proved
more than a restoration for Gómez; it was the embodiment of an opportunity which, in appointed time, made
him the master of Venezuela for a period of thirty
years.

Between Caracas and Maracay they recount stories
that range all the way from the days of the first Spaniards down to the present. The road passes through the
territory most vital for the history of men and affairs.
On one side, an ancient shrine hanging to the mountainside marks the spot where the armies of Bolívar met
and defeated the armies of Spain in the Battles of the
Liberation. On the other side, in a rich-looking valley,
there is a big rambling building, which turns out to be
a rum mill. Those who like to soften things tell you it is
a sugar factory, but as a matter of fact it's a place where
they process cane into sugar and sugar into rum. A sign
proclaimed the rum to be one of the popular Venezuelan

brands. Like most of the drinks made from raw sugar, it possesses an alcoholic strength out of keeping with its harmless appearance. Being cheap in price, it finds a wide local sale.

A little farther along is a rich plantation where coffee, bananas, oranges, potatoes, sugar cane, coconut palms, beans and corn give evidence of the tropical richness upon which the Venezuelan farmer may depend. He has one advantage over the Midwestern farmer of the United States: he knows he is in for a dry season of a certain length and a wet season of about the same period, so he never has to worry about when it is going to rain and when it is going to be dry. The country has developed no weather prophets. The two seasons intercept each other with almost perfect regularity.

We passed a beautiful farm which once belonged to Simón Bolívar. Several generations ago the government purchased it and made it an agricultural experiment station. A number of these training farms have since been instituted by the government; every outstanding agricultural neighborhood now has an experimental farm.

Not far from the Bolívar hacienda is a beautifully developed farm that was the property of Gonzalo Gómez, a son of the late dictator, who now lives abroad. He built, upon a hill overlooking the valley lands, an extraordinary house which had a Turkish look to it.

Gonzalo was in charge of the national lotteries a good many years. He did much for the sports of his neighborhood. One of the features of his farm along this ancient highway is a large cement stadium in which he introduced to that part of Venezuela the great American game of baseball. He brought rival teams and star players and aroused great enthusiasm in the game, which persists and grows.

All along the road you see good-looking farms in the rich valleys which lie in the shadows of tall mountains. They seem well kept. The Venezuelan farm hand gets a nominal sum per day, a house in which to live and a plot of ground which he is free to cultivate for his own use in his leisure time.

As you approach Maracay, your interest sharpens in the things which Gómez built. He had found Maracay a more pleasing place for him than Caracas. He loved simple things, and Caracas frequently made life intricate for him. His great ranch has been taken over by the nation. Some portions of it are used for experimental purposes; other acres are administered under a housing act which has divided the extensive lands into twelve-acre plots, each equipped with a modern three-room house. They are all built after the same model; originally they must have looked as alike as peas in a pod. But the two years that had passed since they were occupied have proved that you may start farmers equal, but they don't remain so.

I counted something like one hundred of these houses, and I saw almost a hundred varying expressions of the care in which they are held. Many of them have re-

*New and old farming methods on a Venezuelan hacienda.*

ceived from their owners a coat of paint or color wash of some kind. Some were blue, some brown, some white, some mottled. I think all the colors of the spectrum were suggested, but light blue seemed to be the favorite of those who used any color at all. Some of the homes had received no attention, and stood as harsh in their cement nakedness as when they were turned over to the new owners.

Most of those that had received a touch of color were surrounded by little gardens with a shaded pathway leading from the highway to the door of the house. You couldn't look at the houses now dotting that part of the Gómez ranch without realizing that in spite of the general and equal provisions of the housing act, the beneficiaries are still individualistic.

These houses are sold to the occupants upon a long-term payment plan. The established price is about two thousand bolivars.

Gómez added much grace and dignity to the city of Maracay. The Jardin Hotel, capable of housing hundreds of guests, and surrounded by gardens, pavilions, clubhouses and bandstands, indicated his desire to build something to exemplify his love for civic beauty. It also proved that Gómez realized the need of better hotel accommodations in Venezuela. He projected, at government expense, other hotels—one at Macuto on the beach at La Guaira; and another one at a mountain retreat called the Hotel Rancho Grande, which was never completed.

It was thought that when Gómez died and the government took its administration back to Caracas, Maracay would die. But while the present administration has reduced the number of soldiers quartered there, Maracay has continued to thrive as the center of a rich agricultural section. The old town house in which Gómez lived is open to visitors, but the place he kept in the country a few miles out of Maracay—which he called Las Delicias—is closed to visitors. One, however, may go and see the zoological garden maintained almost in the front yard of his living place. It is a rather respectable collection of beasts and birds and snakes, kept in modern zoological style and properly safeguarded by the government. One of the outstanding features of the garden is a great collection of fish native to Venezuelan waters. There are, of course, the usual complement of monkeys, alligators and hippopotami.

One of the features of the zoo, pointed out with painstaking care, was a huge lion, declared to be a brother to the well-known Metro-Goldwyn lion which greets the opening of screen performances with its familiar roar. I could be easily fooled by a story like this. The Gómez lion looks almost exactly like the Metro-Goldwyn king of beasts, but since it has never been to the movies, I accept the brotherhood story; but I cannot guarantee it.

☆          ☆          ☆

The ancient highway follows the valley of the Aragua until it joins the valley of Lake Valencia a dozen or so miles beyond Maracay. Then it divides and circles the lake, which is twenty-five miles long and ten miles wide. From there it goes on to the beautiful city of Valencia, turns north and follows another valley through mountain gorges for thirty miles to Puerto Cabello on the Caribbean.

One branch of the road from Maracay goes over the range at the eastern end of the lake some thirty miles to San Juan de los Morros and from there to eastern Venezuela.

All along the road in the vicinity of Lake Valencia are fine haciendas, neat rambling houses, artistically colored, partly hidden in rich fields and saman trees.

Between Maracay and Lake Valencia stretches for a distance of a dozen miles a wide avenue with a touch of Paris boulevard. It passes the elaborate and well-developed lands of the former Gómez estates, the barns and modern stock pavilions which were the pride of his heart, passes the new commercial airport and then comes to a park called Boca del Rio on the shores of the lake. I daresay there is no other park like it in all the world.

They have been carrying on excavations in Venezuela, some of them not far from this lake. It occurred to Requena, a student of archaeology, that it would be a clever thing to reproduce in a public park some archaeological reflections from these excavations. And so they have made an attractive parklike enclosure and ornamented it with concrete figures and symbols of the ancient Indian motifs made familiar by the excavations.

These cement figures are of heroic size and probably create exactly the effect that a man devoted to archaeology would enjoy.

In my judgment, it is the greatest break archaeology ever got in park building.

# CHAPTER III

## *Passing of Gómez* ✓

---

WHILE THE DICTATORS OF EUROPE were tearing up
the treaties of Versailles, rearranging prewar frontiers,
ravaging a barefoot people in Ethiopia, and riding
roughshod over Central Europe, Juan Vincente Gómez,
the most successful ruler of South America, was pursuing an even tenor.

He had been autocrat of Venezuela thirty years,
twenty-seven under the title of president and three years
as vice-president.

He had begun his dictatorship in troublous days.

Dictator Cipriano Castro, whose revolutionary aide
and commissary Gómez had been when Castro upset his
predecessor, had made a mess of things as dictator. He
cherished a delusion still afflicting dictators of the
world that it was honest for the State to confiscate
private property and ignore rights of foreign investors.

While Castro didn't realize it, the delightful fate
reserved for those who strike subterranean lakes of oil
was approaching Venezuela.

There was as yet only a little production. The great capital and engineering capacity necessary to develop the difficult field was hesitant. Smaller investments had been made, particularly in asphalt deposits.

These contributions of capital had reached a point where Castro, who had a petty mind, thought they were worth stealing. He proceeded to violate the contractual rights of all investors, including those from the United States, whether they had put their money in oil, asphalt, public utilities or something else.

He repudiated obligations, both of individuals and nations, right and left—and made war talk.

He was worthy to be an example to the leadership of today in Mexico and Bolivia.

As an immediate result of Castro's crookedness, battleships of Europe, including those of England, Italy and Germany, sailed into Venezuelan waters to enforce the demand that the rights of their nationals be protected and payment made for their plundered property. Venezuela was helpless. She had a few inefficient vessels that could not stand for a moment against even a foreign gunboat. It was an hour when the democracy of the United States wore a shining sword and kept its powder dry.

Theodore Roosevelt was President of the United States. He knew the history and meaning of the Monroe Doctrine. He was able to persuade Great Britain and Italy to agree to withdraw their navies in order that the claims against Venezuela might be settled at a Hague court of claims.

The Kaiser insisted on collection by force and fired upon Venezuelan coast cities. His ships ran up and down the coast, surveying harbors, and obviously planning to establish a formidable naval base at Maracaibo which would control the Panama Canal, then about to be built.

A famous Roosevelt episode in connection with the incident is still remembered. He had asked the German ambassador to come to the White House to receive the formal demand that the Kaiser's navies should be taken away from Venezuelan waters within forty-eight hours. In twelve hours the German ambassador came back to say:

"My master, His Imperial Majesty, does not believe that forty-eight hours are sufficient to permit the withdrawal of the fleet."

Roosevelt shrilled at him, "You haven't got forty-eight hours, you have only thirty-six hours left, and you can tell the Kaiser that I shall order the Atlantic squadron to Venezuelan waters immediately"—which he did. The German government accepted arbitration of all claims, and its squadron sailed away. The incident provided what is known in history as the Roosevelt corollary to the Monroe Doctrine.

The Venezuelan claims were taken to The Hague, where judgments in favor of the foreigners amounting to something over $12,000,000 were awarded.

Castro had been obliged to go to Paris for medical treatment, so when Gómez took over the government of

Venezuela, acting as Castro's subordinate and provisional president, he had to deal with the results of Castro's unwise foreign policy. After a brief period, Gómez concluded that he could do this more effectively with the full authority which would belong to him as constitutional head of the government, so Castro was warned that his health, which might continue to improve in Paris, would probably suffer fatal complications if he attempted to come home. He did make such an attempt, but he found the doors of Venezuela closed to him.

Then Congress elected Gómez to be president in his own right, and he took over the government with all of the liabilities of the Castro regime. Thus he entered upon a career which was to cover twenty-seven years of absolute control.

He announced at once a policy toward foreign investments from which, during the long years of subsequent industrial development, he never veered.

A shrewd bargainer, he established contracts with foreign capitalists for the development of natural resources that were profitable to his government.

Unlettered though he was, it is believed that he was responsible for the oil code under which the Venezuelan government gets more for its share of oil developed by the petroleum companies than do the majority of landowners on which oil is produced in the United States.

Gómez's steady policy not only led to payment of all

Venezuelan obligations to nationals who had been defrauded, but restored confidence in Venezuelan investments. It brought the situation to a point where the necessary foreign capital to establish the expensive explorations and production of oil in Venezuela was attracted. This came at a time when capital, which is extremely sensitive to disturbing conditions, was feeling the first effects of Mexico's attacks upon it.

The first large companies to signify their faith in Gómez's Venezuelan policy toward foreign investors were the Dutch Shell and the Standard Oil corporations.

Before the end of his dictatorship, Gómez had achieved for his country a balanced budget and established revenues that had created a surplus in the treasury.

On the surface there was nothing to worry about, except now and then an incipient uprising of students or social reformers, weary of the Gómez rule. No one thought seriously of questioning the continuation of the Gómez regime.

It was December 1935, and the dictator lay desperately ill.

Maracay, where Gómez lived, was filling up with those who were poignantly interested in the situation which would be created by the passing of the head of the Venezuelan government. It was presumed that the only question which challenged the tense moment concerned the successorship. Gómez's cousin, Eustóquio

Gómez, a sadist, who as warden of a political prison at Puerto Cabello, and later as president of the Andean state of Táchira, had made an unbelievable record of brutality, seemed to feel that he would be singled out to carry the torch of the Gómez leadership. He came to Maracay with a crowd of Andean followers to be present at the last illness of his eminent cousin. There was no indication that a drastic change in the form of government would occur after the grim old man, who had held the situation in perfect control for thirty years, had passed on.

He had written an outstanding chapter in the Latin dictatorships of South America, establishing Venezuela's character for the honesty of her dealings with outside capital, for the payment of all her foreign debts, the maintenance of a surplus in the treasury and thirty years of peace.

He was more Indian than Spanish. He never wore anything but sandals until he was forty years of age. He came from the Andes, where the amenities of life were not gentle.

Some premonition must have existed that a change in the government was imminent. A crowd of young men known as Constitutionalists were there watchful of the procession of events. The key man in the situation was General Lopez Contreras, Minister of War, and the outstanding general of the Venezuelan army.

Eustóquio, evidently alarmed by the presence of so many Constitutionalists, had approached General Lopez Contreras about the successorship for which Eustóquio was known to be ambitious. General Lopez Contreras had reminded him that the Constitution provided for a provisional president to be chosen by the cabinet pending the period when the Congress should meet and elect a new president. Eustóquio had not heard about the Constitution for a long time, and it disturbed him. Later, when the cabinet had chosen Lopez Contreras as provisional president, who removed Eustóquio from the presidency of Táchira, the break came.

The fact that General Gómez had allowed Lopez Contreras to remain in the key position of the government during his last illness is interpreted to indicate that he possibly was thinking of the future of Venezuela in gentle terms. Perhaps Gómez realized, but did not express himself as did Calvin Coolidge, that the direction of government in the new and fast-changing world called for abilities which he did not have. Whatever the cause, Lopez Contreras had been in the Gómez government for a great many years, and Gómez must have known that he was the best man for the successorship. At least the dictator must have realized that Lopez Contreras would not allow the brutal Eustóquio to become the head of the government. Some of the students of history believe that Gómez could foresee the liberalized government that would come to Venezuela under General Lopez Contreras and that for this purpose he was left in the key position during the dictator's last illness.

After Eustóquio received the news that Lopez Contreras had removed him from office as president of the Andean state of Táchira, he thundered into Caracas to demand the head of Lopez Contreras. He dashed up the steps of the government palace, having announced his intention to kill Lopez Contreras as a traitor to the Gómez cause.

A young Spaniard who had suffered torture in a political prison when Eustóquio was warden followed him up the steps, encountered him in a corridor, and shot him dead.

The population went wild with excitement and exaltation. He had been universally feared and hated.

The excited crowd first burned the beautiful automobile which had brought Eustóquio to the palace, then they went upon a mob's holiday, rioting, looting, occasionally coming back to surround the government palace and discuss whether they should tear it down. When they became bored with what they were doing at any moment, they went out and plundered the homes of prominent Gómez followers, members of his family, and other affluent Venezuelans.

This was a picture of what was happening, not only in Caracas, but in every important town and city of Venezuela. Everywhere the immediate members of the Gómez clan were in danger of mob violence.

The army had fired upon the mob in front of the palace when the rioting started, killing men, women and children. Lopez Contreras dismissed the officer who had ordered the volley, explaining that he wanted to keep the bloodshed down to the lowest possible degree.

He had time also to explain to the now thoroughly frightened members of the late dictator's family that he would not protect them from the mob. He would make it possible for them to flee to safety, but if they persisted in staying in Venezuela they could have no guarantee from him touching their safety. Lopez Contreras was criticized afterwards when it became known that he had secretly provided transportation facilities to enable members of the Gómez family to escape, most of them to Willemstad in the neighboring Dutch island of Curaçao, whence they found their way to Canada, New York, France and elsewhere. Some of them returned after Lopez Contreras lifted the ban against political exiles.

The government confiscated all the lands and accumulations of Gómez and holds them in trust under the pretense that they will be needed to satisfy claims brought against the government by former exiles and other political offenders who are asking the government of Venezuela for damages. It was set up as a justification for the confiscation of the Gómez properties that these accumulations should be used to reimburse Venezuela for any damages awarded.

The extent of the Gómez estate, made up as it was of many forms of property ranging from ranches, lands, houses, cash and diverse securities to transportation companies, has never been set forth in actual figures.

Lopez Contreras was taking the lines of least resistance. He wanted to avoid the blood and violence
which mark revolutionary procedure in a country
where a people, long accustomed to obedience to totalitarianism, suddenly finds release and apparent freedom.
So he encouraged the members of Gómez's family and
tribe to leave Venezuela, while he allowed the mob certain latitudes elsewhere in the enjoyment of their new
freedom. His was a sort of planned revolution, with a
guarded outlet for revolutionary passions.

After less than two weeks of looting and bloodletting,
the President notified the mob leaders, who by this time
had become capable of identification, that the holiday
was over, and that no further violence would be permitted.

Having been named President of the Republic for
the term 1936 to 1943 by the Congress, Lopez Contreras
announced that at a certain hour he wished to talk to all
the people by radio. This was a novelty which excited
everybody's interest. In the thirty years he had ruled
Venezuela, Gómez had never made a speech. His most
elaborate public expression did not embrace a dozen
sentences. Now the new President was going to broadcast. It was to be Venezuela's introduction to the radio
voice as a political instrument. They dropped their
looting and assembled at receiving sets all over the nation.

President Lopez Contreras turned out to be an excellent speaker. He talked of his dreams for a free Venezuela and summoned the shade of Simón Bolívar. He promised the people a definite plan for the rehabilitation of Venezuela, this rehabilitation to touch the health, the education and the prosperity of the masses.

He promised them sanitation, new hospitals, new schoolhouses, new transportation facilities, agricultural advancement, restoration of the suffrage privilege, the destruction of political prisons, and amnesty to all political exiles.

It is somewhat revealing of the trustful disposition of the average Venezuelan that the population was perfectly willing to take the new President at his word.

Some labor disturbances then were created by organizers, mostly from Mexico, who came preaching the doctrines of Lombardo Toledano, as modified by John Lewis. They sought to organize everybody, from the bootblacks on the streets to the well drillers in the petroleum districts, into a sort of Venezuelan CIO. They blanketed the entire country with CIO unionism, and finally, to impress the government with this fact, they called a three-day strike, which was in reality a strike against the government.

The government dissolved the strike program by proclamation. Subsequently the Congress passed some stringent laws curtailing Communistic activities and inviting the counsel of the labor leaders in the writing of a modern labor law. This law, which marks advanced legislation, is treated in another chapter.

☆          ☆          ☆

As soon as President Lopez Contreras had announced his plan for the rehabilitation of Venezuela, all the old cabinet members resigned out of generous realization that the new President should have the privilege to select men of special attainments for the larger work the cabinet would be called upon to do.

The Venezuelan program gives every evidence of resting upon the belief that the end goal of society is the creation of a healthy, educated body of men and women trained to render useful service under fair conditions and favorable circumstances.

In their efforts to advance and support this belief, the Venezuelan officials have concentrated their forces for a direct first attack upon disease and ignorance because they realize so clearly that a sick people working under unhealthful conditions not only are seldom able to work but usually have little sustained interest in trying to work. Venezuela's present officials, also clearly recognizing that unlettered and untrained minds are as heavily handicapped in modern life as are weak, diseased bodies, have set out to bring education to a neglected people.

Their first attack in this march along a broad front, therefore, has been upon disease and ignorance. Their second attack will be upon problems of transportation and development of raw materials so that a healthy, trained people may have unrestricted economic opportunities and the nation as a whole may have a sound economic foundation.

The gravest needs of Venezuela today thus might be set forth as:

First, Sanitation,

Second, Education,

Third, Transportation and development of raw materials.

This last, of course, embraces many needs, and its relative place in the categories might well be first, if health did not precede every other demand in this tropical land. While agriculture is the oldest industry in Venezuela, it has made less progress than the others because of the limitations of transportation.

"Education" is not used in the ordinary sense. It includes everything that touches modern living. Many in the population have to be taught the very meaning of the word "sanitation."

# CHAPTER IV

## President Lopez Contreras—His Reforms and His Army

In the tropics the human species matures early. Girls twelve years of age flower into motherhood. At twenty years maturity has arrived with all its cares of middle life.

So Eleazar Lopez Contreras, when he was graduated in 1898 from the College of the Sacred Heart at La Grita with the degree of Bachelor of Philosophy and Letters, was only fifteen years of age. He was not known as a boy prodigy. The next year Lopez Contreras enrolled as a volunteer in the Restoration Revolution headed by General Cipriano Castro. He took part in the campaign of the Andes and Centro which culminated finally in the success of Castro and the occupation of Caracas in October 1899. In this campaign Juan Vincente Gómez was Castro's friend and commissary. President Lopez Contreras took part in all the campaigns of pacification in the country from 1900 to 1903, obtaining by his qualities as an officer all the grades of

28

promotion up to colonel. In 1908 he took an indefinite leave of absence during which he held various civic employments, one of which was as a telegraph operator.

In 1913 he was recalled to service as commander of the garrison group of Ciudad Bolívar. In the meantime he studied military tactics at home and in Europe. He became the best-educated soldier in the history of Venezuela. He is the author of the following military books: *Historic Callao, Synthesis of Military Life in Sucre, Bolívar—Leader of Troops.*

By 1915 he was serving in the capital at Caracas in command of an artillery regiment. Then he was given the post of Sub-Director of War in the Ministry of War and Navy. In this capacity in 1920–21 he was sent on a mission of study to Europe with a side issue to purchase war materials for the army.

In 1923 he was promoted to brigadier general. Unquestionably he was the most promising of all the generals, some of whom were distinguished for their courage and leadership rather than for their literacy.

In 1924 he went to Peru as head of the military mission of the special embassy which represented Venezuela before the Peruvian government in the commemoration of the centennial of the Battle of Ayacucho.

In 1930 he was named the chief of the general staff of the army and held command of the army provisionally until 1931, when Gómez called him to the Ministry of War and Navy, the post he held until December 1935 when, following the death of Gómez, upon the vote of the cabinet in accordance with the Constitution he took charge of the executive power. When Congress met in extraordinary session he was elected President of the United States of Venezuela to finish the constitutional term. At the regular session the following April, the Congress elected him President of the Republic for a term from 1936 to 1943. Nevertheless he initiated an amendment to the Constitution to reduce the term from seven to five years. This was approved, and consequently Lopez Contreras will hold office only until April 1941.

In the cordial interview which President Lopez Contreras accorded to me, he was the very spirit of frankness. I had the friendly offices of Mr J. A. Olavarria Matos, a distinguished citizen of Caracas whose family is connected by marriage with that of the President. Mr Olavarria speaks perfect English, and for this reason the difficulties which sometimes attend an interview between men of different tongues were entirely absent from my conversation with President Lopez Contreras.

The President strikes you at once as an educated, thoughtful man. His years in the army have ripened in him a resource of strength and self-confidence tremendously developed by his studious habit of mind. He would be marked as an outstanding man in any age of Venezuela's history. When Gómez died, undoubtedly

Lopez Contreras was the most capable man in Venezuela for the constitutional presidency. He had never taken part in the controversies that had awakened passion and occasional revolt in the previous administration. He had put down insubordination among soldiers. His impartial administration at the head of the army and his soldierly obedience to the government had given him standing with both staff and soldiers.

"I desired to introduce the discipline of reason to take the place of that of force. Not having a trained personnel in government of this character, I have been obliged to move slowly. I have sought hopeful young men. It has been difficult to find presidents of states and cabinet ministers capable of taking on the grave duties in the administration of a government where so few citizens are trained to public service."

When I asked the President if the response to the democratic form of government had been encouraging, he promptly replied, giving the emphasis of a slightly raised voice, "Yes." Then he added, in a lower tone, "On the average."

"First of all," he said, "I have endeavored to substitute for a discipline of fear the discipline of reason. I have been criticized because I have not been hard enough. I have desired to reach a point where discipline is imposed as a duty to the government not as an ordered thing threatened by stern penalty for disobedience and failure.

"Some criticized me when I took off my general's

uniform and put on civilian clothing. I was the first president to do this. I desired to emphasize the civilian character of my office and build a civic front. They were so accustomed to regard the military as the government that I lost a little of their respect touching the dignity of my office when I put on these," he said, making a slight gesture toward the suit which he had on— a quiet, gray suit, of the effect of which any businessman could have been proud.

It was explained to me that about 5 per cent of the population represents the higher class, 30 per cent the middle class, and something like 65 per cent the laboring and the so-called poorer classes.

"Those," said the President, referring to the 65 per cent, "constitute my leading preoccupation. I am trying to create every facility possible for their education and progressive well-being."

He favored effort to improve the laboring man's position by any legislation that would be really helpful, but made it rather apparent that he did not expect to take radical labor leadership as a political partner in his government.

Amongst other things, he spoke cordially of the cooperative spirit with which the oil companies had responded to his plans for better living conditions in that industry.

He explained that the oil companies already had built over six thousand modern homes for their labor and had added important hospitalization.

He gave the oil companies credit for having fostered a better feeling between labor and capital. He spoke of the influence which had emanated from the turnover of these great organizations, where a large number of workers were constantly going from the employment of the oil company back to the lives from which they came originally, with new ideas of efficiency and new tastes of living.

When I asked the President if he had any apprehension touching Communism, he replied, "Naturally every country is under some fear of extreme modern ideas, all of which, whether you call them Communism or Fascism, lead to the same end."

He believed, however, that Venezuela was not threatened seriously by the growth of either Fascism or Communism. He felt that the philosophy of Simón Bolívar still held the social imaginations of Venezuela.

"We have kept Bolívar as a symbol all these years. Now we hope to begin the practice of his philosophy. My desire is that we may make the symbol a reality in Venezuela."

When I reminded him that Bolívar was not able to make it a reality and died a somewhat disillusioned man, saying "I have plowed in the sea," the President replied that a deeper understanding had come of Bolívar and that thoughtful men of Venezuela in the modern day want their land to become worthy of what Bolívar cherished in his heart and sacrificed in his services.

Calling attention to the general regret men had expressed to me over President Lopez Contreras' statement that he would not stand for another term as president, both he and Mr Olavarria were a little puzzled as to what I meant by the word "stand." When I explained that it was the democratic term men used when they were going to run for office, they were both amused. All President Lopez Contreras would have to do to secure his re-election would be to indicate his desire for it, and the Congress probably would think of no other man.

This situation is so patent in Venezuela that I was not surprised to hear the President say frankly that in some practical respects it might be an advantage for him to stay in office longer than 1941, because the country might be in need of some of the capacities which his experience had brought to him.

"But," he added, "in the long run it would be better for the country to become accustomed to shorter tenures in the presidential office."

☆          ☆          ☆

I visited the Venezuelan West Point, a striking building standing upon a hill overlooking Caracas.

You catch at the institution, as you talk with its director, a spirit of something fine and splendidly patriotic.

The course is four years, and it's a stiff one. It is so rounded out that by the time a student is ready to be

graduated he is entitled to a bachelor's degree as well
as to his military officer's graduate certificate.

In addition to the one hundred students in the various
classes there are forty-eight officers and nineteen cadets
studying military science abroad. The cadets are in
Europe, while some of the officers are in Chile and
Peru. One is at West Point.

When they enter the service they become a part of an
army of thirty thousand men. Much of this army is
quartered in the impressively extensive barracks built
by Gómez at Maracay. Additional barracks, however,
are being constructed in Caracas, the intention being,
as I understand it, to keep about nine thousand soldiers
in the capital.

I was a little dismayed, as I looked about the army
training school in its setting of mountains, to have the
usual thing told me, namely, that they are about to erect
a new building. I hope they will put it off; the old one
is genuinely attractive and seems to be sufficient for the
education of the one hundred cadets, which is its ample
provision.

As I walked through the patio I stopped to look at an
old French cannon which had found its way into Venezuela in 1687. In Latin were engraved, on a bronze
plate sunk into its barrel, these words:

"The last logic of kings."

# CHAPTER V

# *A Democratic Congress and an Unrestrained Press*

I CELEBRATED the 120th anniversary of Simón Bolívar's "libertad" by going to the opening of the Congress at the government palace. This building itself marks a historical note in Venezuela. President Guzmán Blanco built it fifty years ago in just ninety days. He was in a hurry to get it completed for some international event. It must have been as beautiful as a World's Fair dream. It still has its good-looking features, although the hasty construction has begun to show through the years, particularly in the dome, which has accumulated wrinkles.

They always celebrate, as a general holiday, the opening of Congress at the capital of Venezuela, probably failing to realize a deeper truth that has come to older republics, that the real day which should be celebrated in connection with a congressional term is the one on which it closes.

The Minister of the Interior, the most important

36

member of the cabinet and, by virtue of his office, the Premier of the State, occupies one wing of the government palace. Some adjoining rooms with really excellent mural decorations tell the story of Venezuela's fight for liberty against Spain. A great panorama of the battles won by Bolívar covers the dome in a noble room set apart for patriotic memories.

Another part of the palace contains the two houses of Congress, with a corridor running between the Chamber of Deputies and the Senate. There are forty senators, two from each of the twenty states. The Chamber of Deputies is a larger body, selected somewhat upon a representative basis, the size of the membership graduated according to the population. It has about eighty-five members.

The senators are chosen by the state legislatures, while the deputies are chosen for overlapping terms of four years by the municipal councils. The members of the municipal council are chosen by direct voting in a limited suffrage. Those entitled to vote must be over twenty-one years of age, able to read and write, and of the male sex. No woman suffrage movement has yet been started. The Congress chooses the president of Venezuela under a new constitutional provision which gives him a tenure of five years.

The Minister of Education draws 5,000 bolivars a month, with 1,500 bolivars for expenses. Translated into United States currency, this would represent about $19,000 a year with approximately $5,500 for expenses.

This is substantially the salary paid to each of the ten ministers of the cabinet. The president receives a salary of 84,000 bolivars a year, with 60,000 bolivars for expenses. This would make something over $26,000 a year, with about $19,000 for expenses.

There are practically no political or social subdivisions involved in Venezuela's program of social and economic betterment because there are few differences of opinion touching the needs of the social order.

Moreover, there is no general taxation; therefore the so-called taxpayers are not threatened directly in financing the project. The expenses of the government are met chiefly by the customs duties and the oil revenues. The customs duties amount to probably 40 per cent of the total expenditures.

Some of the expenditures for new hospitals and sanitation are being met by the profit of the lotteries, which is devoted entirely to welfare purposes.

If Bolívar, whose impressive figure looks down upon the Chamber of Deputies from a magnificent oil painting, could have attended the opening of the 1939 regular session of Congress, his intrepid soul would have been comforted by the feeling that after 120 years the government of his native land at last had made a big move in his direction.

It was really a good-looking scene. Many of the members, both of the Chamber of Deputies and of the Senate, appeared in morning coats, wing collars and patent-leather shoes.

The two chambers occupied by the Congress are moon-shaped and look very much like the old Supreme Court quarters in the national capitol building at Washington, D.C.

I watched the opening ceremonies in the lower house. There was much embracing amongst the reunited members.

The session began without formality, without prayer. The usual committees were appointed to notify the President and the Senate that the Chamber of Deputies was organized. Then they began to ballot for an acting officer who would take the chair and for men to fill various vacancies in the organization of the body.

There being no political parties, there were no party caucuses. The members voted secretly on slips of paper collected by the tellers, who passed amongst them with little ornate boxes for the deposit of the slips. They reminded me of lodge officers collecting white and black balls.

There was a constant stir on the floor, and the confusion resembled that with which I was familiar in state legislatures.

Newspaper photographers were allowed to come upon the floor and operate their candid cameras. Remembering that no camera ever appears upon the floor of the United States Congress, I mused a trifle as to whether the presence of these men amongst the members was a mark of a greater or lesser civilization in Venezuela.

It was practically a new Congress. Lawyers predominate in numbers and in influence. There are some publishers, a few businessmen and about nine farmers. There is only one soldier in the cabinet—the Minister of War.

Newspapers in Caracas give a broad coverage of world news supplied by the Associated Press to some extent and by the United Press to a much greater extent. These dispatches appear in much the same form as in the United States. But the doings of Congress are reported and commented on by Venezuela's own newspapermen—and they are full of today's freedom. If any libel laws were ever passed to curb their liberty, they were forgotten during the days when the dictator censored the press. It is an unhampered press, and it loves to deal out constructive criticism.

These Venezuelan editors have gifts of wit and sarcasm, and some of their shafts at government officials are barbed with a cruel frankness which occasionally surpasses anything I have seen in forty years of free journalism in the United States.

I kept a translation of press comment on both the Congress and the government, and wondered at times if my press brethren in Venezuela were not overdoing a good thing.

While it is a leftish press, it is not a Communistic press.

A few months after the beginning of the Lopez

Contreras administration, the government was obliged
to deal with some Communists who had come over from
Mexico to help organize the labor along the lines of
John Lewis' pattern, as amplified by the Mexican program. The government, when it wiped out this picture,
provided against future trouble by passing a law to
suppress Communism.

So the new press, being rather well satisfied with the
government program and forbidden by law to espouse
Communistic doctrines, turns its constructive critical
abilities toward individual statesmen. They carry us
back to a period in the United States when even Lincoln was attacked with personal rancor and vulgar
lines. That period of brutal press habit was restrained
finally by a rising public taste in the United States.

In Venezuela, I think, the present situation will improve as the elixir of free speech loses some of its pris-
tine polemic spirit.

Another thought is in the background. These Venezuelan editors are wise in their day and generation.
There is as yet little middle-class development in Venezuela such as gives popular censorship to press standards in the United States. The government is still the
first and last resort in Venezuela, so undoubtedly the
discerning press in that country will know in due time
just where the line of freedom passes the horizon into
the resistance of offended official dignity. They have
lived through a lot of restraint, have these keen Vene-

zuelan pressmen, and here's hoping that they do not abuse too much of their new liberty to make their criticism more free than constructive.

After I had watched the slow movement of the Chamber of Deputies, whose voting proceeded with a leisurely tempo which defied time, I went over to the Senate. Its organization being more or less permanent, the senators were finished with preliminaries. They were making speeches. I have seldom seen manifest more enjoyment in oratory. It flowed endlessly in an unbroken torrent. As I listened, I was reminded of Daniel Webster's remarks to a northern New York audience when he had gone to dedicate a park which contained a great cataract. "No city with a cataract like this," said he, "ever yet lost its liberty."

The justices of the Supreme Court are appointed for six-year terms by the Congress. There are six members, and they are held in high esteem.

There is no jury system in Venezuela. The judiciary is according to the Spanish pattern—the origin of the jury system is Anglo-Saxon, and it hasn't permeated all South America yet.

# CHAPTER VI

## *The President Talks to Congress*

---

THE PRESIDENT'S ADDRESS TO CONGRESS did not come until some days later. I brought home a copy translated from Spanish into English. I shall keep it as a document worthy of a high place in these days when Venezuela is carrying out a most challenging national program.

While the address was being broadcast, I went out into the parks and the streets to see how it was going over.

At Bolívar Square, a loudspeaker boomed forth the message to a few hundred people who were listening gravely and thoughtfully. There was only a little applause. The workmen along the neighboring sidewalks who were putting in the new water-works mains did not even stop to lean upon their shovels.

Through the business district, where the loudspeakers could be heard, I saw little groups of men listening in silence. Out on a hill in a park in front of a famous

Catholic church there was a loudspeaker but not a
single listener. Sometimes in a store or office I saw a
few people huddled before a receiving set.

This small audience did not indicate a lack of respect
or of enthusiasm. It was the stolid indifference of masses
who have been touched only lightly by the thought of
self-government. They gathered in great crowds along
the line of the streets which the President traversed,
with military escort, on his way to and from the government palace. More of those attracted by the cavalcade
were looking at the soldiers rather than at the President!

The reception accorded the speech indicated more
clearly than anything else the expressionless characteristic in an uneducated population.

There was a spiritual quality in the message of President Lopez Contreras. Coming from the head of a
government in which Congress had, for too many years,
been a negligible quantity, he gave what must have been
an assuring expression to the Congress in these words:

"The executive comes here as a collaborating entity
which does not demand from you instruments of unrestricted support for its determination and initiatives,
but rather a patriotic co-operation free and autonomous.

"I have always aspired to live, in my country, the republican life consecrated to its institutions. Elevated to
the position of head of the Nation, my first act in that
high position was to return to the Republic its political
decorum and legal rights, creating the regime of
legality in evidence today. Towards this I have lent all

my support and authority, constituting myself as its constant guardian and stimulating with word and example everything that has contributed to strengthen such a position."

The President made terse reference to the fact that although given the power to govern by force he had preferred to govern as head of a state of free men.

He referred to the fact that, in the midst of two ideological currents shared throughout the world to-day, his government had maintained itself firmly in the position of austere republicanism. He took occasion to deliver a broad hint of his latent powers, referring to the opposition of contrary bands which had subjected him to bitter attacks.

Only a little more than two years before, he had invited the exiles to come home, giving amnesty to all who accepted his administration and pledging an honest adjudication of every personal right.

He had kept this pledge, but now he was warning some of the discontented that likewise he had kept the power to protect himself.

After exposing for a moment this steel in the gloved hand, he expressed a grim faith that his policy of conciliation, "keeping before us as a constant guide the spiritual unit of the Republic," would succeed in an hour of "dark forebodings for humanity in dictatorial lands."

Then he delivered himself of the pledge against any possible establishment of totalitarianism:

"I shall use all my vigilance to free this people from the doctrines expressly prohibited by our fundamental charter, and which soil the conscience of a good part of the world. I shall continue to combat, as I have up to now, by force of persuasion, by preachment and honest advice, employing only when it becomes necessary those arms which the law gives me for the defense of our social rights, of public order and the reasonable principles which govern our lives."

Plainly in this, the most important deliverance he had made to the Venezuelan Congress, President Lopez Contreras was seeking to impart a serious realization of the maturity that had come to the most exacting of his problems. While young when measured by time, many of them had grown old to him through hours of pondering over their compelling presence.

You cannot read the President's message without a deep respect for his desire to inform the people about the exact state of the nation. It seemed to be the utterance of a dreamer turned realist under pressure.

He told them about the eleven agricultural training schools which had been opened, as well as the higher schools to train agricultural teachers, veterinarians and experts in husbandry. He mentioned everything from bee culture to botany, dealt with cattle ticks, fisheries, forestration, encouragement of new population and establishment of agricultural colonies.

After he had presented an amazing catalogue of Venezuelan activities he came finally to the labor question, where he spoke of the improvement in the conditions of work, in living conditions and wages, and dealt with the intense action relating to health, hygiene, culture and education in the labor world.

He made the significant statement that "the good intentions of the government have been twisted by Marxist tendencies which have filtered into some of the labor associations, lifting these out of their natural channels to throw them into class struggles and toward social revolution."

He asserted that "the laborer has found governmental support for such of his claims as have been believed to be just."

He spoke of his encouragement to the organization of unions "which seek through their solidarity the proper defense of their moral and material interests, cohesion within the union, their professional perfectionment and intellectual uplift."

Then he added, "Unfortunately demagogy, operating under cover, has disturbed this sane purpose, perverting with its propaganda the motives that inspired the idea of association to convert the labor organizations into fighting elements, into bodies of reaction against the State, against our institutions and against other social classes, especially against those who rather than being enemies should be their allies, the employers. Incorporated in the unions, the efforts of the Marxist elements have been concentrated upon pushing the worker towards political strife, placing him on the road of the contingencies which politics must of necessity bring about. It is therefore a patriotic duty to co-operate with the government in the sense of trying to rid our workingmen from this rebel leadership and separate them from that path so full of dangers."

Having developed this intensely frank criticism of the radical labor leadership, he then made this ultimatum:

"To consider our interests not from the point of view of selfish individualism but from the vast panorama which the entire collectivity covers, even in its minutest parts, must be the slogan of all who struggle for Venezuelan reconstruction."

Before his audience had recovered from this startling iconoclasm, he hit them with another fresh viewpoint. "I wish to speak to you," said he, "about something that has nothing to do with material tasks, but which lives in the mind of us all and is the fruit of an educational design of the present regime; we refer to administrative honesty, of the diaphanous conduct of the man in public service, of procedure that can bear the scrutiny of all, of probity as a norm for official actions, of the new atmosphere which we breathe and in which governors and governed alike feel more assured."

He closed with an utterance worthy of a man standing in Bolívar's shoes:

"The hour in which we live," said he, "is one of renovation. The world has witnessed it. We are present as actors at one of those great stages of history when a new human conscience arises and in which new concepts replacing the older ones yearn to find expression in the political structure of the nations. . . . In tune with this universal rhythm, Venezuela sets its course, respecting at the same time its patriotic, religious, domestic and civil traditions."

# CHAPTER VII

## *Limitations of a Latin Democracy*

---

IT WAS UNUSUAL to be in a political atmosphere in which prophecy is mute.

One day, visiting with a group of Venezuelans, prominent in social and governmental life, I said, "What's the gossip about the next presidential possibility?"

The deep silence which greeted the cordial inquiry stung me.

"Listen," I expostulated, "if I had propounded that question to a group in the United States, I would now be dividing time amongst the citizens eager to discuss the possibilities."

I couldn't get them started.

They hadn't been accustomed to giving thought to matters of this kind. No political mind existed. No line-up had emerged. There were no parties, no candidates, and none of that dash of thin political sound waves which beat upon the shores of our abundant life in an hour like this.

Digging in, I sought to develop a candidate.

"How about the minister of war?" I said. "He's an attractive young man. Will he be a candidate? . . . What's the matter with the excellent Ambassador Escalante? Wouldn't he make a good president?"

I got nothing out of it but uneasy absence of sound.

When I was leaving, a courteous Venezuelan, feeling that I might misunderstand the restraint, said, "Don't worry over who will be the next president. The subject is being given proper attention. Whoever it is, the government will continue to depend upon Lopez Contreras for a long time. He wants to retire as president, but he'll still be General Lopez Contreras of the army, with a power to veto any unwisdom that may come to us out of our immaturity."

This restraint is the political accompaniment of every country where over 65 per cent of the population isn't as yet conscious of any reason why they should vote, and by virtue of the educational qualification isn't eligible to the suffrage. In the United States frequently 50 per cent of the eligible voting population doesn't take the trouble to go to the polls, but makes its contribution in a more or less intelligent vocal interest in men and measures, adding to the flux of democratic thinking.

Sentimental writers have built a picture of "Juan Bimba," the Venezuelan symbol of the average man. Obviously he isn't ready to contribute anything to the democracy.

But he isn't forgotten, as five thousand new schools, big and little, established for his education, testify.

Venezuela may increase in democracy as Juan Bimba increases in education and understanding.

The essential strength of Venezuela is in its Constitution as guaranteed by Lopez Contreras, his able cabinet and the Congress.

The limitation on suffrage may sound a little undemocratic, but it is immeasurably better than that government which Pendergast gave to Kansas City or the Long brothers gave to Louisiana.

It is a little difficult for those cherishing the United States type of democracy to reconcile their hard and fast conceptions of the institution with that of the South American states. We started out with different traditions, establishing our democracy in a land of Anglo-Saxon patterns where the people were more or less homogeneous. There was a low percentage of illiteracy and a high sense of personal responsibility amongst our early pioneers. The burning conviction of our pioneers was that they were capable of self-government and that no government was worthy that did not have the consent of the governed.

When democracy came to South America, it was necessary to establish a pattern that, while cherishing the rights of the governed, could take their consent for granted, so far as the large percentage of the population was concerned.

The Latin states of South America, with the exception of Brazil, possessed Spanish forebears who represented centralized government to the *n*th degree. The Conquistadors were not only the conquerors of the country, they were settlers and colonizers. The land was owned by the State and was parceled out in the form of land grants. The basic population was Indian, and there were no modern ideas amongst the Spaniards of educating the masses.

Then came Simón Bolívar preaching democracy. His democracy could not embrace quite the latitude of the Anglo-Saxon institution because there was a lack of homogeneity in the units of the population.

After Bolívar had freed the Latin states from the rule of Spain and contemplated the masses who must be welded into republican governments, he realized that the populations of these newborn republics were composed of illiterate Indians, a small percentage of proud Creoles, and some ambitious generals who controlled very largely their own armies. Hence they had to create a type of administration that would fit a badly balanced civilization so far as the possibility of a universal suffrage was concerned.

Many makeshifts were employed. Dictatorships became the commonest way of switching the government from the hands of one crowd to another.

Bolívar himself, who had no doubts as to the fundamental principles of democracy as they guaranteed the quality of government, realized that at the moment government in South America could not rest upon the consent of all the people. I am told that there is on record a copy of the constitution prepared by him for the Republic of Bolivia which he thought might become a model, although it was never adopted. It provided a limited suffrage based on education, with life tenures in certain of the commanding positions of the government. Thus Bolívar sought to provide a stability that might meet the fluctuations of the temporary dictatorships.

It should not be forgotten that we have had our doubtful moments in history touching the capacity of general suffrage. Alexander Hamilton, who was the spiritual founder of our republican form of government, believed in limiting mass influence by a system of delegated authority.

That which stands out today with very comforting clarity is the fact that all of the Latin-American republics have written constitutions which contain ample guarantees, so far as language can go, of the inviolable rights of the people. Even where dictatorships have appeared to render these guarantees meaningless, they have left a sense of obligation growing stronger as the populations of the various republics increase in understanding and education.

None of these Latin-American republics has been without frequent periods of honest, able and relatively free government. The thing which the modern Venezuela is trying with promising success to accomplish is to raise the 65 per cent of her population, known as the poorer class, to an educated status, to improve their health and to give them the Western viewpoint that the most useful and honest career is that of intelligent labor. Industry has suffered in South America from the attitude of the Spanish gentry that physical labor is demeaning. This led to a neglect of trade and technical learning. Universities had heavy registrations in literature, law and kindred professions, but only slight registrations in engineering and technical courses.

The unusual educational activities now going forward in Venezuela, and which I have sought to set forth with some conviction, mark the effort to enlarge what might be called a middle class in Venezuela.

During the 110 years since Bolívar, there has been a constant decrease in the government of dictatorships and in the importance of the armies as a stabilizing force.

In Venezuela, for example, there are only two full generals left, one of whom is Lopez Contreras, under whose command as president the army is being taught to cherish at its professional obligation loyalty to the government and not to an individual dictator.

The twenty Latin-American republics which emerged in 1824 under the direction of the liberators have been gradually finding their way toward a real pattern of democratic government. Some of them have well-thought-out federal systems of government in which the nation exercises those powers specifically delegated to it by the constitution while the remaining powers are re-served to the states.

In other republics the centralized form of government has been adopted. In several of them measures of social legislation touching old-age pensions, unemployment insurance, wages-and-hours regulations were in vogue before they were adopted in the United States. The saving characteristic of them all, even when they have been practicing dictatorship, has been their pretended adherence to the principle of democratic government.

I observed at the Pan-American Congress in Lima, Peru in 1938 that most of the delegates and news reporters from the United States were looking for Communists, Fascists and other evidences of totalitarianism. They were worried by the specter of European dictatorships. Apparently Hitler himself misunderstood the opportunity of the Pan-American Congress. He thought that the field was open for a discussion between the merits of totalitarianism and the democracy of Pan-Americanism. Germany had more reporters at the conference than did the press of the United States, and they flooded the news services with their copy.

Mexico had given the picture a touch of Communistic realism, and for a little while the fear was general that Mexico's confiscations would appeal to the South American states. It didn't take long to discover the fact that there was no sympathy in the Pan-American Congress with Communism.

Something much more serious than confiscation was involved in the Mexican incident. The Mexican government had not only stolen invested property, which had been done before in South America, but it had sought to justify the theft by the introduction of Communism which threatened not only those who were the victims of confiscation but likewise those who were its beneficiaries.

At the Pan-American Congress little attention was paid to Bolivia, which had just seized the properties of an oil company, because Bolivia had not sought to make the confiscation the foundation for establishing a totalitarianism borrowed from Europe. It was plain theft.

The Lima Conference marked the steady growth of the Pan American Union from the loose formation from which it started in the days of former Secretary of State James G. Blaine to the excellent co-ordination expressed in the Lima declaration. Today that statement, in the light of the new war's events, becomes a pact of American solidarity whose strength will not be questioned anywhere in the world.

One of the things which confused our understanding of the South American situation was the presence in some of the republics of large German populations and what appeared to be the superiority of German trade relations. We did not realize that the Germans who have been building their own business lives in South America are somewhat like the Germans who contributed to the melting pot in the United States. They

are individuals before they are nationalists. As business
agents they have outsold us in many places in South
America not only because they had made a better study
of the customs and the languages of the South American
people than the United States exporters had made, but
because they had established easier terms for the liqui-
dation of mercantile accounts than we had established
and because they often resorted to subsidized price cutting to undersell American products. While we had no
easy terms we were frequently easy marks.

The German was seldom victimized; his Latin customers generally took the obligations of a German account more seriously than those of a United States
account.

There always has been considerable discussion of
both the Japanese and Italian penetration of South
America. That there is a large Italian population resident in South America is a notable fact, and some ner-
vousness has grown out of the establishment of a
Caproni airplane factory in Lima. However, the Ital-
ians have blended with the population in a peculiar
way, and while they cry "vivas" to the name of Mus-
solini, their devotion has no fanaticism that threatens
a national issue. The character of their trading, outside
of airplanes, has not interfered very much with American exports.

The Japanese, outside of the advantage they are gaining from the Mexican situation, have not become menacing as a political problem. As a competitor in trade

they enter certain fields with goods that reflect the cheap labor situation in Japan. This is particularly true of the disastrous effect they have had upon cotton and other textiles. They imitate many of the American products and sell at a cut price. A great bulk of their exports, however, is made up of trinkets and trashy articles. They have contributed little to the contest for the trade in durable goods. On my way home from the Lima Conference I stopped at Guayaquil the day before Christmas. The shops were full of Christmas offerings, 90 per cent of which were trinkets from Japan.

The criticism of the inadequacy of our business representation in South America does not extend to the splendidly organized corporations, such as the Pan American Airways and the transportation companies, the mining companies, the petroleum companies and other successful institutions that have trained international forces. It applies only to the vast number of concerns in the United States who look upon the South American territory as a field subject to experiment in which volume may be stepped up. They have not taken it very seriously. They have not, in fact, realized how tremendous a feeder of international business the South American field makes possible if properly developed.

It is strange that we fell down in this respect. The tremendous increase that came to our South American business in the World War should have led to the careful cultivation of the field. However, in the years which immediately succeeded the World War there was plenty of business at home, and apparently we did not take seriously the matter of our South American trade connections. Now war has again thrown South America into the lap of the United States, so far as supplying her necessities is concerned. The displacement of European goods by American goods will begin at once. The opportunity ought not to be ignored by the business interests in the United States. The occasion provides for an interchange of good will and permanent benefits that should bind the two Americas in a mutual relationship of faith and self-interest.

From 1914 to 1917 our foreign-trade boom carried our annual volume of exports from $2,365,000,000 to $6,290,000,000. Our exports to South America as well as our imports from there more than doubled as our goods displaced foreign wares.

It isn't often in a trading nation like the United States that the door of opportunity opens a second time, as it now promises to do, as a result of the present European conflict.

It should not be understood from this implied criticism that we have lost the South American market. We have merely failed to take full advantage of it. During the last twenty years the United States has enjoyed nearly one third of Latin America's total export and import trade. Our Latin-American export figures for 1937 were $639,422,000, while the import figures stood at $705,000,000. Our export figures would have been far less favorable except for the fact that our road-building equipment, agricultural implements and mining machinery are all preferred in South America not only because of their sturdy character but because they are made for heavy use. In respect to the activities employing this machinery South America deals in North American sizes more than she does in European sizes.

We have more than held our own in the increasing airplane business of the Hispanic states, and our future in this direction could not be better than it now is. Electrical appliances, radios, sewing machines, modern office supplies all have a justified lead.

The Monroe Doctrine may not be much better understood than in the days of the President who gave it his name, but it is less misunderstood. We have now in both Americas a clearer comprehension that the doctrine is neither a pact nor a regional agreement between the United States and other nations. It simply expresses a principle of the foreign policy of the United States uttered at a time when South America was threatened by the invasion of European forms of government. The Pan American Union, which has grown up as a potential confederation, is after all the legitimate child of the Monroe Doctrine in its modern understanding.

Our ministers of good will should not be confined to trade relations, important as good trade connections are in the building up of a cordial spirit. Most Reverend James H. Ryan, Bishop of Omaha, recently suggested that one of the most useful things we could do would be to revive the Pan-American Congress of Journalists.

Latin-American newspapermen should be invited to the United States and made better acquainted with North American life. An exchange of editorial courtesies between the journalists of the two Americas would clear up a lot of misunderstandings which grow in an atmosphere lacking the comprehension of immediate contacts.

The Germans have built in Berlin a Hispanic Institute containing a research library of Spanish-American literature and history. It is said to be the most comprehensive in the world. The educational leaders of Germany have used this along with exchange scholarships to bring many Latin young men to Germany.

Certainly there is every reason why the United States could cultivate a special movement in the direction of these friendly relations.

Germany has improved her relations in South America with a radio broadcast established under the pretense of a news service. It is given free to the South American newspapers. It has many excellent features of a news service. It is shot through with propaganda, and the warmth of its interest in South America has made a friendly impression. I would not suggest that we copy that type of appeal, but certainly, with all the modern services of transmission, we could establish a new and effective approach to these American neighbors.

A recent improvement in the instrumentalities of mutual contact was the establishment in the Library of Congress at Washington, D.C., of a Hispanic Room which will be developed into a thorough historical museum and library of the Latin countries.

Occasionally some educated young person in the United States asks me about the opportunity for employment in South America. In several states in South America, where industry is thriving, there are exceptional opportunities for trained young men from the United States. Venezuela, for example, needs engineers, office administrators and technicians of the sort which the training schools of the United States turn out in abundance. But there is no natural opportunity for anyone from the United States in Venezuela unless, in addition to his other training, he speaks the Spanish language.

There are many great United States corporations in South American republics which run training schools of their own to teach the Spanish students the English language. It has become, so far as the trained occupations are concerned, a bilingual country.

The very first element of preparation for a student contemplating service in Latin America is a working knowledge of the Spanish language. A well-educated young man from the United States, speaking only the English language, would have about the same show at a job in South America as a South American, speaking nothing but the Spanish language, would have in searching for employment in the United States. In Brazil, the largest South American republic, the language is Portuguese.

# CHAPTER VIII

## *The Melting Pot of Venezuela*

---

THE POPULATION OF VENEZUELA, now on its way to be 4,000,000, is made up of pure-bred Spanish 5 per cent, Negroes 10 per cent, Indians 40 per cent and mestizos, mostly Spanish and Indian, 45 per cent.

The Spanish pure-bloods have been beating a slow retreat. The melting pot has absorbed them slowly for generations, and that pride which goeth before the fall has weakened under the pressure of the majority movement, which has been toward racial admixture.

The belt in which the Negroes and mulattoes are most numerous is on the coast lines. They have come from the various islands of the Antilles, from Cuba, Trinidad, Haiti, Puerto Rico, Jamaica and Panama.

They are the contributions of ancient slavery days, the building of Caribbean activities, including the Panama Canal Zone, and other industrial labor pressures which for years have either brought them by force, in earlier days, or attracted them by circumstance and easy opportunity in later years. They are dock laborers, field hands, workers in casual employments. Occasionally a mulatto gets to the front with an unusual display of brains, which after all are more important in Venezuela than in most places, but the mainstay of the population is the Spanish-Indian mestizo. The mixture produces a simple industrious individual, capable of great development in labor callings, educational pursuits, engineering and all the arts that are useful in civilization.

As you go west toward the Andes Mountains, the people take on the qualities of mountain folk in every clime. They are more rugged in physique and bolder in an independence of spirit and direct action. They have a leadership similar to that which has come always from the mountains to all people.

The Andean region in modern years has given Venezuela many of its leaders. Gómez and Lopez Contreras were both products of that high country, as were most of the other lieutenants of Gómez's government.

Efforts have recently been set on foot to affect population by immigration laws. The Chinese have been subjected to a limited exclusion act. By a process of selectivity, they may now come for agriculture only. Those who had been in business in Venezuela recently have been transferred into agriculture. They ran small places —lunches, bars and barbershops. They worked hard, made money and sent it to China. It was the steady flow of their money to China that finally called attention to them and brought the edict that if they wanted to stay in Venezuela they must farm the soil and eschew business.

Few Japanese are here. They have not yet become a problem. There are only two Japanese stores in Caracas, and there is no Japanese exclusion act.

Negro immigrants from the Antilles are now prohibited, although of course they have a right to admission from all states that are members of the Pan American Union. There is growing a social color line so far as the Negro is concerned. He is being gently retired from the army as officer material.

Although not as large as in most South American republics, there is a good-sized German population. You find Germans in business everywhere. In Caracas, many of the older and wealthier families are Germans who yet hold their citizenship in the Fatherland.

On a fete day recently, when every residence must display a flag, I found in Caracas the crooked cross of the Nazis flying in more numbers than the flag of any nation save Venezuela. This doesn't mean necessarily that these residents are Nazis. Many of them are not.

Recently there has been an increasing number of petitions from Germans for Venezuelan citizenship.

Something over 150 German Jews came to Venezuela under the Refugee Agreements as agriculturists, but since the agricultural opportunities in Venezuela did not appeal to this group, it is understood that the experiment will not be repeated.

The population has received some recent accessions

from planned colonies of immigration, as at "Mendoza" and "Chirqua," both farming projects for the encouragement of agricultural immigration. There was originally installed a contingent of 536 Spanish immigrants, at the second a colony of 237 Danes.

The greatest source of new population, however, is abundantly reassuring. Venezuela is doctoring its sick people and protecting children from tropical pitfalls. The loudest cheer that greeted any portion of the President's message to Congress was at the paragraph in which he told them that infant mortality has already been reduced 50 per cent by the modern movement toward sanitation and hospitalization.

This is humanitarian service of the highest order. No state renders finer service than when conserving its most precious of all natural resources, the lives and health of its men, women and children. Not only is Venezuela doing this and doing it as well as any other country, better even than most, but she also is attempting to capitalize fully on this invaluable natural resource by training it for effective citizenship in self-government, by instructing it in the ways of the world and in the methods of earning a living and in encouraging it to render useful, constructive human service.

# CHAPTER IX

## *Over the Jungle by Air to San Cristóbal*

A NEVER-TO-BE-FORGOTTEN AIRPLANE TRIP which was to last five days took me from Maracay south to San Fernando on the Apure River—then west to the Andean foothills near the Colombian border, where the airship was to leave me on a plain which, God willing, will someday contain an airfield. Then I was to make my way to San Cristóbal, some forty miles from the landing spot, then back to Ciudad Bolívar, along the northern and eastern coasts of Venezuela across the tremendous Delta Amacuro. Having encompassed this encircling of central, western, northern and eastern Venezuela, I was to go west again and south to the headwaters of the Orinoco River and into the distant territory of the Amazonas.

The journey was over two ranges of towering mountains, broad, high plains almost vacant of human life, some jungles that literally steamed. In the latter, from the plane, I saw many forms of animal and vegetable

68

life. Deer frightened by the plane overhead could be seen running away from the banks of the river to some adjacent forest. Alligators wallowed in the swampy pools or rolled about in muddy rivers. Tapirs, tigers, leopards, scared from their haunts, made their way to forest places where they could escape the threatened terror of the giant monstrosity that had disturbed their jungle solitude.

Below us we could always see swarms of aigrettes, more decorative in their native air than ever they were in the days when fashion wore them.

Orchids of every variety clung to the jungle trees, adding an unbelievable touch of beauty to a scene as unreal as a jumbled dream. Nothing is more difficult to realize than the beauty of the orchid clinging to the tall trees of a thick forest or an impenetrable jungle. The general impression prevails that the orchid is a parasite flower. As a matter of fact, nearly all the members of this family grow and thrive upon the trunks and limbs of trees in midair, simply clinging to a single stem or small limb and therefore quite properly called "air plants."

On the afternoon of the first day we landed, after a trip of some eight hundred kilometers, upon a virgin airport at San Domingo. There was a thatched hut, but the only thing that distinguished the landing place as an airport was a large pile of gasoline barrels holding a reserve gasoline of super-octane content.

Major Alcides Quintero, Venezuela's most famous

pilot, set us down upon the unprepared field as gently, it seemed to me, as though we had been landed on a cement runway. It was a strange place, primitive to the last tropical degree. However, a new Lincoln Zephyr automobile was waiting for us, and we started over a mountain road, still under construction, for San Cristóbal.

The hardy citizens of this region, characteristic of mountain folk everywhere, have given to Venezuela some of its outstanding leaders. Eleazar Lopez Contreras was born in Queniques, in the Venezuelan Andes, on May 5, 1883. Gómez had come from an Andean village not far away. The Andean people stand out for their ruggedness and self-reliant qualities.

All along the way we slowed down to maneuver a passage through workmen who were chiseling the road in the mountain foothills and building bridges or culverts across canyons and smaller rivers. Someday this road will be as beautiful a scenic route as any mountain country affords.

Game so wild that it did not fear an automobile remained in plain sight. At one place we had to stop the car to let a monkey get out of the road. He was not afraid of the motorcar; he had ideas of pedestrian rights which characterize more cultivated highways. He tottered around on his hind legs deliberately, like a child who has not learned to fear the traffic. The shrill honk of the driver's horn, which awoke mountain echoes, didn't disturb him. Finally he waddled off with incomprehensible composure, erect, with a forearm held straight up, as though he were directing traffic.

As we proceeded into a more level country, herds of cattle, better-looking and more numerous than any others I had seen, were grazing in the lush grass of these Andean foothills.

Finally, as we approached San Cristóbal, we passed a cultivated spot which a sign proclaimed to be "The New Agricultural Experiment Station." This was one of the numerous schools established within the last two years by the federal government, now making a super-drive for the education and encouragement of agriculture.

Then we dropped from the high country into the surprising city of San Cristóbal. The governor of the district told me it held a population of thirty-five thousand. Two hours later, in the office of the president of Táchira, of which this was the center, the statement was made that the city had forty thousand people! It is a growing city. In a beautiful valley with mountains sixteen thousand feet high, looking down from the Andean range, it has never had any oil revenues. It was built on agriculture, but like every other place I had visited in Venezuela, it was enjoying a business boom.

Here, too, the present public-works program has emerged from the paper stage. The young governor of the district, José Trujillo, who was born here, spent the afternoon and until long after dark showing me the new improvements, after which we went to have dinner with the president of the state of Táchira, a cultured man, not much over forty, of whom I had frequently heard. Dr Abel Montilla had served Venezuela as minister to Czechoslovakia, Mexico and Chile. After twenty years of absence from the turmoil of Venezuelan life, he was recalled from diplomacy to be president of a state which had known little serenity.

Táchira had been governed for a number of years by Eustóquio Gómez, a cousin of the former ruler. Both as warden of a political prison at Puerto Cabello and later as president of Táchira he had distinguished himself for his cruelties. It is undoubtedly true that many of his excesses were blamed upon his powerful cousin.

The contrast with the recent past was impressed upon me as I listened to these young men of the new government who grow emotional over modern plumbing, sanitary units, children's schools, libraries and works of progress.

Governor Trujillo, at home, would be the president of the Chamber of Commerce and a moving spirit in the Rotary Club, perhaps the district governor. He started off by telling me that San Cristóbal has no insoluble social problems, no unemployment, no relief set-up for employable persons, and that the town is happy in the feeling of an undisturbed prosperity.

He was enthusiastic about the new agricultural schools where students of agriculture are taught the use of modernized machinery. American farm tractors have come here to stay. Modern mechanism hasn't invented a gadget for the use upon farms, big or little, that hasn't found its way into these agricultural schools within the last few months.

An expert in animal husbandry told me of the plans on foot for improvement of the livestock breeds. The director of the Production Department of Agriculture said that already the influence of agricultural education had increased the coffee crop until the production expressed itself in figures running toward 4,000,000 pounds. Improved cultivation of tobacco had increased the crop and led to a processing activity that expresses itself in cigar makers and cigarette manufacturers.

The increased food production was what gave the governor the largest satisfaction. Said he, "We now raise enough beans for our own consumption," adding, "We never did that before." He told me that, under more intelligent cultivation, more sugar than the state needed was being grown. While he was on the subject of sugar, he detoured long enough to discuss the practice of processing sugar cane into rum.

"The overemphasis of rum production isn't good for our people," he observed, and added that reduction of rum consumption was being sought by the imposition of a special tax to make it less attractive to the poorer classes, who buy it so cheaply that they consume a great gallonage of it.

The governor drove me out to see the new modern packing plant just completed. It helped to explain the new road over which I had come that afternoon. Over this highway will be brought cattle from the rich pastures adjacent. The new plant will have a capacity of ninety beeves and fifty hogs a day.

The small packing plant is a new type of industry in Venezuela. Formerly there was only one packing plant. Now in several cities small plants are being completed, refrigeration is being installed, and the ordinary by-products of the packing industry are being manufactured, all of which adds to Venezuela's capacity to produce its food supply.

The governor went out of his way to drive me over a bridge, just completed by a French engineering firm, above a handsome river which separates the main city of San Cristóbal from an exclusive-looking suburban town.

He told me of the new straw-hat factory being completed and of the minerals which geologists were now rediscovering. Then we started in on the new school-houses, hospitals and sanitary units.

I had already been told in distant Caracas that the states in the far regions, even in the Andean mountain regions, were keeping pace with the extraordinary development in sanitation and education which stand out so conspicuously in the nation's capital.

In San Cristóbal a modern, well-equipped sanitary unit has been opened in which all the preventive practices of the United States have been introduced. Experts have visited the hospitals in our country and in other countries, bringing back not only the latest methods but

*Transporting sugar cane in Venezuela.*

equipment, that place the system of the new combined clinic and maternity hospital and visiting nurses entirely out of the beginners' class.

"We are in a hurry," said the director. "We waited a long time for this." He said that in San Cristóbal in two years they had decreased infant mortality by 50 per cent. "If we keep this up," he said, "in another three years Venezuela will be ranking as the most healthful state for children in South America."

The unit has six visiting nurses working under the direction of a trained nurse from Panama. They have modern trucks rigged up for carrying on their routes medicines and accommodations for emergency work. They have established a school to teach visiting nurses. Over two hundred people now come for examination, diagnosis and treatment. To the poor all medicines and treatment are free.

A quizzical young doctor remarked that it was the only institution in Venezuela in which there might be noticed an increase in poverty.

"The simple people achieved the notion that the poor get better treatment than the paying patients, and this has added to the popularity of being poor," he said.

A source of great satisfaction in San Cristóbal is the new city library, which has become an important center of education. It is a beautiful colonial building of really exquisite grace, built by the government, which fortunately employed an architect who was a real genius. The structure and its equipment cost 1,000,000 bolivars.

It has reading rooms for boys, classrooms for special instruction, gymnasium, theater, ample accommodations for books and general reading rooms, and a room for student organization.

The broad culture of the institution goes far beyond the usual activities of a library. It is really the community center for the new intelligentsia of Táchira.

Local pride, now the fastest-growing thing in a land of feverish accomplishment, pointed out to me that the beautiful marble and shining hardwood with which the building is trimmed were all of native production. One might write for hours about the educational progress of this little city, but the statistics tell a vivid story.

In three years they have established two hundred new schools; twenty-five hundred more boys attend the public schools than before. There are night schools for parents and adults all over the state. In a little school free lunches are served. Domestic science is being taught in all the schools, in an effort to add to the battle for better health the element of better food for the masses.

The hospital, Vargas, was the last project we visited before we went to the president's dinner. It is a general medical center, enlarged recently to contain four hundred beds. It is well equipped and apparently well conducted, and notwithstanding the fact that over one hundred beds were empty, the authorities were getting ready to build a new 500,000-bolivar hospital.

"Where will you get the money?" I asked.

"From the lotteries, of course," came the reply. There are in this state 127 free hospitals, big and little, supported to a greater or less degree by the lotteries. The governor wasn't enthusiastic about it, even though every dollar now goes to maintain the hospital and sanitary service. He was of the opinion that the general influence of the lotteries was bad. He was in favor of cutting the drawing down from three per week to one and ultimately pinching them out altogether.

Before going to the president's dinner, I was taken by the governor to the social club of San Cristóbal, an exclusive place, artistically furnished, where San Cristóbal society puts on its best. It costs five hundred bolivars to join this club and 12.50 bolivars per month to maintain membership, but you could see that the membership fees and dues had not crippled the membership list. As I thought of the bankrupt social clubs all over the United States, my appreciation of the spending capacities of this favored land increased.

Later in the evening, at the president's dinner, where I met some leading citizens, they added to my personal observation from their experience and philosophy. In the party were men who had spent interesting years all over the world. One of the guests told me that one of the places I had missed was a manual-training school where men were being taught to make rough serviceable shoes out of native cowhide for a population eager to take off sandals, and even more for thousands who had always gone barefoot.

The opinion was expressed that the importance of teaching these people to wear shoes, and of providing them with footwear at prices they could afford, was equal in its civilizing effect to education. The range of discussion brought out how profoundly some of these Venezuelans are dreaming of applying the money they now have to the social ideas they are so eagerly adopting from abroad—all to aid the culture of this population which must be raised to modern standards if it is to be worthy to share in the economic advantages of a land just awakening to such abundant opportunities.

The subject of crime came up, and the governor said that in four months not a single criminal case had developed in San Cristóbal. He offered to get the records to prove his astounding assertion.

Another guest asked if I had been apprised of the mineral resources. When I admitted that I had missed that, I was told that deposits of all valuable minerals were known to exist, including gold, silver, copper and iron. The lack of transportation was given as the reason that the knowledge of these deposits, through the years, had meant nothing to them.

These men said, with pride, that they didn't even need oil. Then in a few moments the fact that oil symptoms existed there, and that an oil company had recently established headquarters in San Cristóbal to explore the field, started them on new dreams of what a subterranean lake of oil would mean, if added to their other resources, now that roads are being projected and the new air transportation had broken the long-existing barrier between San Cristóbal and the Venezuelan centers. They were so enthusiastic about this that later, as I went home, they drove me past the place where the new airport was being built in an effort to close the gap between San Domingo, where I had landed, and San Cristóbal. They told me of loans by the federal land bank to farmers and for the building of houses for workers on the installment plan—upon which there is a visible start in an impressive colony of new houses. It was the only enthusiastic and unanimous discussion I had heard of that subject for several years.

We had to get up at three o'clock the next morning to drive back to catch the plane, but it was twelve o'clock before these men finished the alluring story of the new San Cristóbal. The president himself was to take the early plane, and when I caught him secretly stifling a yawn, I knew it was time to go.

It was still dark when we started the next morning to retravel the menacing mountain road back to the airport. How many narrow escapes we had, I do not know. I surprised everyone by going soundly to sleep, and two hours later, when I awoke, we were there.

Another plane had arrived during the night. I discovered this to be a photographing and map-making plane sent out by the government to make a chart of the region. I thought of the recent past when that rugged land was fully four weeks' travel from the government seat.

## CHAPTER X

# *A New Order in the Distant Guayana*

---

Bound for the distant Amazonas, we retraced our flight of the day before as far as the San Fernando airport, then went south for a high swift flight over the Orinoco River, until we came to Atures, the capital of the federal territory of Amazonas. It was a very new town under a very old name. The Spanish priests, since the days of the Conquistadors, had known it, but for four hundred years it had slumbered in primitive contentment, responding indifferently to the efforts of kind-hearted Franciscan monks who had established a mission and sought to lure the tribes to adopt the puzzling ways of civilization.

Gómez, after a few efforts to establish his government in this remote spot, had dropped the project because of the strength of a native chief who lived off the land as a feudal lord, levied contraband, robbed commerce, took slaves, practiced polygamy, and shot up the country roundabout with blowguns and bows, whose arrows were tipped with hammered iron. His raids extended into Colombia, where his fierce attacks and savage fighters made him rather a dreadful figure. When Lopez Contreras took over, he sent a force sufficient to stop the marauding and take charge of government.

So when the airplane set me down at Atures, civilization still looked a little rough around the edges. The native Indians, who constituted the mass of the population, were vastly entertained, puzzled and curious. A priest explained with pride that, using an ax and a scythe, he had made the airfield upon which we landed!

The Indians swarmed on the landing field, eying the plane with greater interest than they did the distinguished visitors who had just appeared in their midst. Before I left they warmed up socially, gave me a blowgun, some arrows and a chieftain's headdress and showed me other courtesies not usually bestowed. They even offered a beautiful leopard's skin, which I declined because of limited transportational facilities.

A Franciscan monsignor with a most benignant face stood amongst his native charges, and they appeared to be better satisfied with life than most humans I've met.

The land was beautiful. The place held a curious suggestion of some of the first efforts of the early West of the United States to catch up with the East. There was a new state house, which looked a little like some of the ambitious courthouses of the early days in western Kansas. The territorial government didn't have need of a large building, but in that primitive spot the two-story boxlike structure just completed to house the administrative offices loomed like a pyramid.

The simple, low-built school buildings with wide openings were in charge of Monsignor. With glowing face, he showed me the schoolhouse for boys, and the modern equipment, some of it from the United States. There was a dormitory center for over fifty boys with schoolrooms on each side. He introduced his prize pupils, who shook hands with the heavy gravity of Indians going through a rite. I met the baseball team.

Monsignor took me to his manual-training shop where, with modern machinery, he was teaching Indian boys how to make the simple practical things in daily demand. He knew every piece of machinery in the shop, and every boy. He was priest, mechanic, teacher, father to the members of this lonesome tribe and worthy ambassador of a gentle Christ.

I asked about medicine and sanitation.

Immediately a good-looking white man stepped forward, Dr M. A. Wendehake, "Inspector de Sanidad." He was an interesting, well-educated man who had served the cause of health in Colombia and other tropical countries.

He told me of the simple first duties of his profession, which were to teach people how to wash their teeth, use modern toilet facilities, and keep clean.

It was difficult, he explained, when the old system of travel by overland from Caracas to the Orinoco and by river to this outpost had required thirty days. Now by airplane the trip could be made in two days. Although the plane came only once in two weeks, and the cost of a ticket to Caracas was 216 bolivars, it gladdened the soul of this doctor to realize how much closer he was to a center of modern life if he should need emergency help in getting anything from Caracas.

The doctor, who was not communicative about himself, was gravely serious about his work and gave me copies of his last report to his chief, the Minister of Public Health, about the steady progress. He left me with a feeling that his spirit of service was akin to that of Monsignor.

I was introduced to a teacher of agriculture and expert in animal husbandry who expressed the determination of the Contreras government to lose no time in the work of agriculture. He had arrived before agriculture in this remote and lovely land.

The memory of the cup of coffee which I had received in San Cristóbal at three o'clock that morning was getting blurred, and I was wondering if food were included in the modern reforms, when a governor's deputy arrived and told us a lunch had been prepared in the officers' quarters, a long, low, competent-looking building near the state house. Here the assembled personnel of the government made an impressive appearance. They were all young, mostly Spanish-Indian mestizos. They looked eager and alert. They were all experts at something, and college graduates. The lunch was not elaborate, but it will not soon be forgotten. A great platter of ham sandwiches, made with United States crackers, turned out to be as good as they looked. The hosts served champagne, in proper champagne glasses, and beer to those who preferred it.

My traveling companion, René Borges de Villegas, an important government official who had become my guide, interpreter and fellow enthusiast, and whose moves I always followed, took beer. I went along with him. When later I asked him why he preferred beer to champagne, he told me what imported French champagne cost in the Amazonas, and I was glad I had not laid a new problem upon the economic treasury of the country.

Then we were taken in an automobile to the river and shown the rapids of the Orinoco. The car was, as usual, a new one from the United States. Out near the edge of a forest, by the riverbanks, we came to a clearing with a good-sized thatched native house and a priest in charge.

"This," said our guide, "we call the luring post."

He explained that in the outlying forest, jungle and mountains were many members of a fierce tribe of Indians who could not even speak the Spanish language; some had difficulty in understanding the language of neighboring groups. The effort was to lure these tribesmen out of their fastnesses and get them reconciled to modern life. This house, with native converts on guard, attracted the curious-minded savages of the neighboring forest. They came in to look things over, and finally they were persuaded to stay and try the white man's medicine.

It would be vastly easier to let this corner of the land drift along, following nature's bent, but the government is making a definite project of reclaiming the Indians into the active known population and teaching them to work. Much thought in Venezuela is directed to the increase of population, and the shortage of labor gives impetus to the effort to enroll the sixty-five thousand Indians of this region into some sort of productive relationship with the white man.

My guides told me more in detail of the Motilone Indians, who occupy a unique position in the Andean region. These constitute a savage nomad tribe who fire with bow and arrow upon oil workers in the region of the Colombian-Venezuelan borders, where important oil explorations are going forward. The Monsignor took particular pains to tell me that none of his Indians belong to this tribe, and there is no disposition in the wild tribal people amongst whom he had labored for thirty years to do mischievous and murderous things. Then, with sorrow in his voice, as of a father speaking of wayward children, he told me how mean and inexplicable the Motilone Indians are. Said he, "They shoot poison arrows at the operatives of the oil companies." He told me this two or three times and mused over it, saying, "I can't understand it."

When I told him that in New York City people were also shooting poisoned arrows at the oil companies, he was puzzled. When I left him, I could see by the look in his eye that he hadn't yet gotten the point!

Nearly everybody in the Department of Geology and Geophysics who does work in the field in the region of the Venezuelan-Colombian border has a story about the Motilone Indians.

One of my companions told me of a personal experience while he was exploring in this region. One day he left in his camp a package of money wrapped in canvas—he was carrying it to another oil camp for payroll purposes. His camp was unguarded for a little while; when he came back the Motilone Indians had stolen the canvas in which the money was wrapped and left the money.

Physically, the members of the tribe are powerful. Their skill and effectiveness with the bow and arrow are not to be treated lightly. They use a six-foot bow with a long arrow made of hardwood sometimes dipped in native vegetable poisons. They use the weapon like a catapult, sitting down, putting their feet against the bow and pulling back the cord with both hands. Their arrows have been known to pass entirely through the body of a victim.

Some of the companies are providing their engineers and scientific explorers with mail suits manufactured in New York by an armorer who makes sixteenth-century equipment for masquerade purposes. The shirts are sleeveless and fall a little below the hips of the wearer.

I talked with a young graduate in the geophysical

work from Oklahoma. He was exploring in the region of the concessions along the Colombian-Venezuelan border where these Motilone Indians lurk constantly. He told me he had been advised to get one of these mail shirts. They are made of aluminum alloy, lined with light cotton muslin, and weigh only six and a half pounds. He had decided not to wear one.

"When the tropical heat gets busy with you," he said, "six and a half pounds are not to be ignored. None of the boys in our camp wear them. We feel that by being watchful and keeping guard around the camp at night, we will be able to take care of ourselves.

"Living down here," he continued, "has a peculiar effect upon you. At first you are worried about everything. The stories about snakes and spiders bother you. When we came we didn't dare venture out of our tents at night until we had put on heavy boots. Now sometimes we go out barefoot!"

Recently some members of the oil personnel, attacked by Motilone Indians, picked up a wounded child belonging to the tribe and are taking care of him. When you become acquainted with the skill of the oil-company training schools in teaching the Indians the tricks of the oil trade, the prophecy that this young Motilone may someday come back and be a geologist in the field of his tribal fathers is not absurd.

The first activity of the Motilone Indians was in the Barco Concession. The oil-exploitation rights in the Barco Concession are owned by the Colombian Petroleum Company, which is in turn owned by the Texas Corporation and the Socony-Vacuum Company, two outstanding United States oil concerns.

Since 1938 the Colombian Petroleum Company has been building a 263-mile pipe line. The company is to discharge its oil in the newly developed Caribbean port of Covenas. The project has cost $40,000,000, of which $18,000,000 went for the pipe line and the remainder for the development of the oil wells.

The 263-mile pipe line began flowing in October of 1939, with a 25,000-barrel production daily, which will be increased gradually to seventy thousand barrels. Sixty-nine productive wells have been already produced. There are two storage tanks of eighty thousand barrels each and an additional one of fifty-five thousand. A small refinery at the new port can handle about five thousand barrels daily. The new oil will go to South America and western Europe.

The successful development of the Barco Concession is another example of Western capability. Colombian politics, tropical disease, the towering Andes, the death that lurked in the jungle, all delayed the work. Freight airplanes carried 11,000,000 tons of freight over the mountains for the development of the work—for which suspension bridges 350 feet long, tractors and concrete mixers were needed. The pipe line which has been built from these new oil fields at Petrolea on the Colombian-Venezuelan border is another victory for the petroleum engineers, who have overcome mountains and jungles and brought the Barco Concession to a successful operation in spite of high mountains and Motilone Indians.

As we waited a half-hour at a more or less temporary landing field in the Andean foothills, Señor Borges introduced me to an attractive young Spaniard who revealed that he was a prisoner in the neighboring concentration camp recently established by the government for those who violate the law against subversive influences.

The camp was near by, although not in sight. There were about a dozen inmates who had been confined there under the Anti-Communism Act. There was no need for a fence around the camp. The prisoners were given all the individual latitude they cared to take. They could escape into the Andes on the west, though this was dangerous for many reasons—no roads, no food, bad water, Motilone Indians. They could go into the jungle to the east, but it wasn't safe. Every poisonous insect, snake and beast of prey kept ward over it.

So they were loafing, cherishing their Communistic notions and working on each other. They were utterly uninterested in the humane program being worked out by the social-minded government of Venezuela. They didn't care for the government; the government didn't care for them, but it kept them alive.

When I suggested to one young man that maybe there was a common meeting ground for himself and the government of Venezuela, he quoted Karl Marx. He was a nervous youngster whose wealthy Spanish parents had spoiled him. He had never encountered an economic problem in his life. Whether he spent his time in a concentration camp in the Andean foothills or in the more tensely developed society of Caracas doesn't matter much to the world, but I was interested in the case of this abnormal young Spaniard who had lost all his moorings.

When I said to Borges, "What's the matter with him?" Borges replied, "He's crazy."

Maybe, after all, that's the answer. Borges himself is a student of Marx, but it hasn't unsettled his reason.

At San Fernando, on the Apure, I encountered the first note of economic discontent.

In a seat in front of me on the plane sat a Venezuelan traveling salesman who had gotten on at Nutrias. He talked to me over his shoulder, opening the conversation with the declaration that he regarded Franklin D. Roosevelt as a modern Abraham Lincoln. Touched by his compliment to our President, and not wishing to be outdone in courtesy, I replied that I regarded President Lopez Contreras as the modern embodiment of Simón Bolívar.

The traveling salesman had his own ideas about Lopez Contreras, which he revealed, just as I had my own ideas about the modern Abraham Lincoln, which I concealed.

With the salesman it was a case of puzzlement. He

didn't understand Lopez Contreras; he is a "middle-of-the-roader." With Gómez, now, there was no delay about finding out what he was going to do.

"You went to bed at night wondering. In the morning you woke and it was all over," said the salesman.

I told him we also had a President who could make sudden moves and who possibly had more of the Gómez technique than that of the more cautious President Lopez Contreras. This set the salesman off on the topic of Gómez, and we never did get back to the subject upon which the conversation had opened.

Later I talked with a merchant at Ciudad Bolívar who had operated the alligator industry on the Apure at San Fernando. He had made a fortune at it, in spite of payments to the government. He said his turnover in alligator hides sometimes ran into 600,000 bolivars a year. Unlike the traveling salesman, he didn't blame Gómez for the destruction of the alligator trade, laying it to a thing I had heard mentioned at home, namely, "the depression."

At San Fernando, however, the Venezuelan boom had not arrived. The cattle industry, which gives first importance to the place, still languishes. One thing for which San Fernando waits is better transportation.

San Fernandoans were deeply interested in the present government program; the day I visited the city they were looking for some government engineers who were coming to study both the transportation problem and river control.

Unusual courtesies were afforded me at San Fernando. I was taken to a good-looking house with a tropical patio. With all the grace of a Spanish welcome, I was told that the house was mine. Down at a restaurant the Chamber of Commerce gave me a dinner. The warmhearted cordiality brought out a sense of the really friendly relationships that have come to characterize the attitude of Venezuelans toward citizens of the United States.

I had to leave San Fernando early the next day, so I arose at six o'clock. When I came from my walled patio to the street, I saw a crowd of workmen at a building a few doors off. It was a new government hospital, and the workers were administering their own daylight-saving rule. They worked eight hours a day, so if they went to work at six in the morning, they didn't have much of a job left after lunch.

I said good-by to the nice little house, surrendering it back to its owner, who, I later discovered, was the Bank of Venezuela, which had a mortgage on it.

# CHAPTER XI

## *Unsolved Mysteries of the Gran Sabana*

---

Tentative objections were raised when I first suggested that I should like to explore the Gran Sabana.

This wide expanse, which stretches across Venezuela south and east of the Orinoco and embraces much of the giant state of Bolívar—itself as large as Texas—is a land of traditions. Many students of geology and climate say it holds the key to the greater future of Venezuela. Its potential riches, inaccessible because of lack of transportation, undeveloped because of lack of population and of capital, are becoming better-known by reason of the surveys and investigations of the Lopez Contreras government. Capable of sustaining millions, it has only a few thousand people, mostly Indians living under primitive conditions.

Visitors seldom go there; writers have viewed it from afar.

The President of the Republic hesitated about my trip, pointing out that the rainy season was nearly due

93

and that the high winds which developed in some sections preceding the rain often made flying uncertain.
The President told me he was about to recall, for the
present, the geological commission then making a survey there, out of consideration for the safety and comfort of its members, for the duration of the inclement
season about to begin. But apparently he caught some
of my enthusiasm, for he suggested that I talk it over
with the Minister of the Interior. The minister, who
was most responsive, sent me to the army air service.
The army air chief thought we had better take it up
with the aero-postal service, whose trained pilots had
already established some travel routes there and knew
the possible landing places and not only the facilities
but the difficulties of flying in the sparsely settled
region.

Finally the army air chief, the postal air chief and
the Minister of the Interior were one on the project.
They really gave me more than I had requested.

The proposed flight delighted my soul, for it would
take me over great mountains, plains and jungles and
into the region where both diamonds and gold are said to
abound. The aero-postal chief combined it with one of
the regular trips that go weekly as far as Tumeremo, in
the gold fields. He makes an occasional trip of about
three hundred kilometers south, as far as Santa Elena,
six miles from the Brazilian border. He would make
some wide detours for my benefit.

And so one morning, with my heart in my mouth, I

set out with René Borges. We started from Ciudad Bolívar with the good wishes of Dr Ovidio Parez-Agreda, president of the vast state of Bolívar, who came to the airport to see us off. We flew over rivers that looked black from the air, jungle forests that seemed impenetrable, and bits of valleys that shone like emeralds in their little pockets amongst the mountains. The flight provided a topographical view of an uninhabited country which will remain in my mind for a long time.

Finally the valleys recurred with increasing frequency. We landed in two hours at Tumeremo, a good-sized town adjacent to the gold fields. Our landing field was one made by nature. Man had interfered only casually. A metal-roofed hangar and a large pile of gasoline barrels identified it as the new municipal airport. The plane comes once a week and is an event in the remote land where other travel is slow.

People had gathered by the time the plane stopped. Many Indian women, who wore large gold earrings and other ornaments of pure yellow gold, were in the crowd. Some of the men wore gold nuggets on their neckties or coat lapels. By this sign I would have known that we were in the gold fields.

The governor of the district was there to meet us and invited us to come back for the night, as accommodations were uncertain at Santa Elena. The pilot figured that he could complete the round trip before dark. Night flying would be impossible, as there were no floodlights on the natural field. So he gave us a fast ride over what is perhaps the most beautiful country I have ever seen. Rolling plains that looked as fertile as those of Iowa stretched over the horizon—plains rich with grass, watered by small rivers and dotted by the flowering trees and palms of this incredible land, which is tropical in its latitudes and natural scenery but possesses a bracing temperate climate due to its altitude.

About halfway down to Santa Elena we stopped at the camp of the government geologists. They were the only geologists ever to visit any part of Venezuela who were not looking for oil.

Dr Freeman, an eminent authority from Puerto Rico, was in charge of the group. One of the Venezuelans is a graduate of Stanford University, another of Colorado University at Boulder. They were all full of hopeful prophecies about the Gran Sabana as a future agricultural dependency. Some of them talked about it with the excitement in their voices which I imagine may have characterized those United States pioneers who talked about Oregon and other far Western agricultural lands which were even more remote from transportational facilities than the Gran Sabana is today.

I met here Jimmy Angel. I had heard of him frequently since arriving in Venezuela. He is a notable American flier who, following a lust for adventure had come to Venezuela. Attracted by the stories of gold in the Gran Sabana country, he made flying explorations.

He had discovered a cascade over three thousand feet high, where the great volume of water dissolves into mist before it hits its water bed. I saw this from a distance. It looked like a silver band streaming down a mountainside.

Jimmy stunned Venezuela by bringing his plane down on top of the legendary Auyuntapui Mountain. It is the tallest in its region, being nearly ten thousand feet high and towering over the rolling savannah. The Indians had woven around its flat top many superstitions. According to old legends, the mountain guards, in its innermost recesses, the fabled wealth of El Dorado, which the Spanish Conquistadors always sought.

Auyuntapui had for generations been called inaccessible to human feet, and there was a legend that all who had ever tried to climb it had perished. A story persisted that one American explorer had reached the top, found rocks of pure gold, and died.

All this was too much for Jimmy Angel, and so on October 9, 1937, the day being clear, he started out at eleven o'clock in the morning on the fateful journey. He took along his wife, who was an enthusiast, both about flying and about Jimmy. A friend, Gustavo Heny, and a peon, Miguel Delgado, accompanied them. Jimmy invited the Spanish explorer, Cardona, to go along, but Cardona had once flown over the flat top of the mountain and said it would be too dangerous. A landing, in his judgment, would be practically impossible.

Jimmy had a good plane which he had named the

"Rio Caroni." By twelve o'clock he was circling around the mountain, and soon he found the top in a clear atmosphere and brought his plane down on what looked like a good landing space. The plane proceeded smoothly for a little way; then a wheel sank thirty inches into the mud, causing the plane's tail to rise in the air and its nose to dig in.

Before landing, Jimmy had cut off the gasoline to avoid accident to the motor. This precaution saved the plane from fire, because in landing one of the oil lines was broken and the gas tank was damaged so that it leaked, and there was a dent in one of the wings; but otherwise the plane was as good as ever when Jimmy finally abandoned it and started out with his companions on a twelve-day journey down the mountainside to reach his Indian camp at Camarata. The mud was so deep on the top of the mountain that they sank to their knees in it. They had spades, but they couldn't dig fast enough to keep on top.

For days government planes searched for Jimmy's party, and their friends mourned them. Then, when the story of the plane had been added to the legends of those who had perished on Auyuntapui, word came that Jimmy and his party were safe in Camarata.

Jimmy's story of his twelve-day journey down the mountainside is a classic. It rained continuously. The precipitous path provided slow, hard going. Jimmy says that he saw the decendants of every bird and every animal that Noah had with him in the Ark. The birds, never having been disturbed, were so tame they could be fed out of hand. Jimmy reported that the wealth of the subsoil was incomparable, there being clear evidences of iron, gold and other minerals. He was convinced that this mountainous district had untold riches, but he didn't have any plan for getting them out! He believes he found on his journey down the mountain the richest gold mine in the world, but his marks of identification now elude him. He makes search for it at odd times, but he has not been able to relocate it.

Jimmy's party had carried to the mountain enough supplies to feed them on the way down, but on the ninth day the hardships of the trip caused them to abandon their supplies, and they finally arrived in Camarata in the last stages of exhaustion and hunger.

When I saw him, Jimmy had another plane and was employed as a flier by the government for the geological commission, where his knowledge, daring and flying ability fit into the work of the young enthusiasts who search out the truths of the Gran Sabana.

I was told that a project was imminent in which Jimmy was to be an important figure. He was to be given a commission to organize a border patrol to stop Brazilian gold panners from secretly panning the Coroni River and its tributaries, in whose swift waters both gold and diamonds abound.

I found when I met Jimmy that he was an old friend. In 1923 I had known him as a test pilot of the Travel Air factory at Wichita, Kansas.

I left the geological camp with regret. It was an impressive body of enthusiasts who, in my judgment, are blazing a trail which may lead to an economic independence as important for Venezuela in its way as are the petroleum deposits.

But I was still miles from Santa Elena, and the sun was two hours past the meridian. So we made a swift start, and for the next two hundred miles I saw unroll beneath me a country of surpassing pastoral beauty. That some of it is too dry in the dry season and too wet in the rainy season, no one can doubt. But most of it is tillable and productive, as was proven by the fact that at the very end of the long dry season it was green with lush grass, free from the wiry fiber that infests so much of the pasture lands north of the Orinoco.

Finally looking down upon the swift-moving plain I saw a flock of sheep, a few horses and then some cattle, all in their isolation giving sudden reality to this agricultural paradise. Then three houses came into view, and I knew we would soon be circling to land at Santa Elena, where an Indian mission is located and a lone white man has set up the outpost of modern civilization, in a well-developed ranch.

We could see the Indians hurrying to be at the landing. When we had come to a full stop many of them stood off in half-frightened wonder; some, suddenly seized with panic, ran away. To most of them an airplane is a live thing. Pilots told me that in the regions of the Indians they must guard the plane night and day. These children of nature pry around to see if they can't find an airplane egg which they can purloin and maybe hatch themselves an airplane. The first time I heard this I regarded it as a joke, but finally I accepted it as a sober truth, no more unreal than countless other strange tales told in this strange land.

A nun accompanied by a dozen clean-looking Indian girls came up and presented her placid charges, who were models of deportment. These Indians had been lured from the plains and forests into the mission's activities; and in addition to the mission, the government itself is taking an interest in them.

In a few moments a lean, dignified white man, burned browner than an Indian by the tropical sun, arrived on horseback. He was Dr Lucas Fernandez-Pena, the man of Santa Elena, a well-educated Spaniard who spoke English. In a way he was both discoverer and pioneer of the place. Twenty-two years before he had penetrated into the entrancing land and decided to make it the home of his generations. He married an Indian woman who gave him seven children, six of whom he had educated under his own tutelage. The youngest, a shy good-looking boy of twelve, came up at his father's bidding and shook hands.

"I've decided to give this lad a better chance," said the father fondly. "I shall send him to finish his education at Caracas." Caracas wasn't far as the crow flies, but when I thought of the rivers, jungles and mountains I had flown over to reach Santa Elena, it seemed like a journey to another world.

I asked Dr Fernandez what he could raise in this part of the Gran Sabana, and he replied that everything he had ever planted here grows. He spoke of his rice, cocoa, wheat, corn, beans, sugar and potatoes. He raised simple things of food value, the processing of which was comparatively easy. He had found the grass nutritious. His cattle, sheep and crops had done well. He produces more than he needs and feeds the Indian population, but lacks market facilities for the realization of the full opportunities of the ranch. His livestock has to be guarded against tigers, so far as possible. For a period of ten days before I arrived, an animal had been killed each night.

As Dr Fernandez told me of the fight he was making to protect his cattle from the tigers of the Gran Sabana, I recalled a story related to me in the Apure valley by a ranchman who occasionally lost an animal to a boa constrictor. The huge snake does not at first encircle the body of its victim, but fastens himself upon the cow's back and stays there until the terrorized animal has run herself to a point where she has no resistance left. Then the snake makes its kill by crushing her.

Nothing more serious than his fight with animal life seemed to burden this wise Spanish gentleman who had built himself a retreat in a faraway place, only to find, twenty-two years later, that the world had discovered him and was asking him all the curious questions by which civilization makes its presence known.

I thought he looked a little lonesome when I bade him a hasty good-by in order to satisfy the pilot, who must make his several hundred kilometers back to Tumeremo by sunset. The doctor wouldn't see another plane for a month.

Here, within the shadow of the equator, there is no twilight. When the sun sets, the day is done; the pilot kept telling me to hurry.

On our return trip we had to stop at the geological camp for gasoline. Here a German engineer and his assistant attached to the geological expedition took a seat in the plane to ride north.

The mayor of Tumeremo had assured me that a special dinner would be waiting at the local hotel when I returned; had even asked which I preferred to drink, champagne or whisky and soda. When we returned, the mayor met us at the plane, which the pilot, with surprising gentleness, set down upon the prairie sod of the airfield, just as the sun went down. To get there he had flown the last fifty miles at a speed of over 260 miles per hour.

As the mayor of Tumeremo drove us from the airport in a handsome new United States car over what one might, with considerable courtesy, call a natural highway, I was constantly comforted by what he had said touching the special dinner. For one thing we were to have venison. We paused at the city square, where I sat with the mayor and his party for an hour, listening to the stories of the gold rush of some fifteen years before, when the gold and the diamonds were first discovered in the rivers of that neighborhood. It had been a real gold rush. The richest mine involved was for a brief period a famous producer.

The mayor discussed the modern mining situation in the field. He is still engaged in gold mining as a side issue. He thrills to recollections of the "richest gold field in the world." He finds the gold-mining adventure profitable even now. He grubstakes the ambitious ones who go into individual mining. With naïve frankness the mayor explained that he supplied these individual miners at a sufficient profit to allow latitude for considerable bad bookkeeping on the part of the miners, upon whose individual reports he must depend for his share of the gold they obtain from their crude efforts in his mine. He knows he is being mulcted, but his effort is to get an approximate result from the game as he plays it, making the profit on the supplies absorb the loss of gold stealage. He said that it was the established system, and many of his fellow citizens were playing it that way. He was serene, easy-going, and apparently well satisfied with general returns. He was providing a profitable labor for hundreds of individuals, and he knew enough about the quality of his mine to be able to safeguard himself against too generous a betrayal of his confidence by those he grubstaked.

He reviewed for me, with local coloring, the history

of the famous controversy with Britain over the neighboring boundary between Venezuela and British
Guiana.

I met the "Inspector of Borders." Here, within a few
miles of the Brazilian frontier, he must be on constant
guard against the citizens of the neighbor country who
make free with the rivers of Venezuela to pan for gold
and diamonds, and who, in spite of the vigilance of
border guards, carry away considerable wealth.

The mayor of Tumeremo then took us around to the
hotel where presumably the dinner awaited. Our arrival
astonished the good woman who runs the hotel. It developed that she had mistaken the German engineer and
his companion for my party. They had arrived an hour
ahead of us. She had given them our dinner! It was the
only serious case of German penetration I encountered
in Venezuela.

The next morning I flew over to the gold-mining
fields at El Callao where the New Gold Fields of Venezuela, Ltd., which is an English outfit, mines 70 per
cent of the gold now being produced. The other important operating company is French—the Compañía
Francesa de la Mocupia. While these two large companies mine the principal percentage of some 20,000,-
000 bolivars' worth of gold reported annually from the
Venezuelan field, it is estimated that at least twenty
thousand individuals in this neighborhood make their
living panning for gold. Occasionally they find diamonds. The profit from this activity is much greater

than appears in any reports. There is no organized industry behind it, but the diamond merchants of the world send their buyers to this field.

My traveling companion, Señor Borges, had told me that I should carry away from this field both gold and diamonds, and he made his word good, bringing me, before we left, enough pure yellow gold in nugget form to make a twenty-dollar gold piece—if I wanted a twenty-dollar gold piece—and a little black diamond which made up in brilliancy what it lacked in size. His uncle, Señor Hector Villegas, was in the gold business when Señor Borges was a boy. Borges was full of the stories of his uncle's day. One of them was typical of the period. His uncle used Indian assistants. Two of these assistants were expected to bring from a remote river district a shipment of gold. After a period of waiting and concern, one of them arrived in a dreadful condition. Weakened by several days of travel through the jungle and across the wilds, he explained that he and his companion had started for headquarters, having secured a rich recovery of gold. The boat met with an accident, sank in deep waters, his companion had drowned, and the gold was lost in the bed of the river.

Señor Hector Villegas knew Indians and had upon them a strange hypnotic effect. So when finally he demanded of this poor draggled creature the true story of his adventure, repeating constantly with impressive sternness, "Where is my gold?" the native finally broke down, confessed that he had murdered his companion, who had been a lifelong friend, sunk the boat, buried the gold, and started across the distances to tell the story which he had fashioned out of whole cloth. He took Señor Villegas back to the place where he had committed the murder and hidden the gold, which was recovered.

I met Mr Boyd, the American manager of the English gold-mining company, whose crisp American vocabulary had probably been enriched a bit by his recent experience as manager of some English mines in Mexico. He had been having it out with the leaders who were applying the "labor squeeze" to the mining situation in Mexico.

His mining camp here presented a fine picture of efficiency. His many workmen were housed in modern homes, and the delinquencies in commissary supplies, natural in that remote place, were balanced by careful attention to the importation of the necessities of life for men engaged in arduous work. The manager told me that if it were not for the unfavorable exchange rates, the field in which his mines were located would constitute the outstanding gold discovery of the world.

He referred to the fact that when the new mining company opened there, the exchange rate was from five to seven bolivars for a United States dollar. Then the dollar had been depreciated to fifty-nine cents, and so the exchange rate is now only 3.19 bolivars for a dollar. Mr Boyd explained that, therefore, to meet the high exchange rates they had to confine their mining to the richest ores which offer the only opportunity for a profit. Under the old exchange rate, they could secure a sufficient gold content from the lower-grade ores, which now cannot be profitably handled.

I realized, as I talked with Mr Boyd, that you have to go away from home to grasp the grim reality that a United States dollar is worth only fifty-nine cents.

The defense of the Venezuelan economists who insist upon keeping the bolivar on the old gold standard —not the new gold standard, but the pre-New Deal gold standard—is that Venezuela is an importing country, and that in an importing country it is desirable to have a high-priced dollar. They realize, of course, that it, in combination with the tariff, has played havoc with their cost of living and has been very detrimental to their exports, including coffee, bananas, hides, etc. To meet that havoc, even if somewhat ineffectually, they have established subsidies for agricultural exports. To justify the high-priced living, they point to the new labor laws and high wages. This answers for those twenty thousand Venezuelans who get the high wages of the oil companies and the forty thousand or more who have government employment on the new works, but it does not reach the masses, more than 50 per cent of the population, who must subsist on agriculture and casual labor and who, while benefited by the boom, still find it difficult to keep up with the daily demand of the high living costs.

The figures given me by the superintendent of the

gold mines indicate the real strength of the gold-mining possibilities. Under the present arrangement, in spite of the deterrent effect of the exchange rate, they are known to be producing $10,000,000 worth of gold a year. Considerably more would be added to this if the record of all the gold panned by individuals were known. As it is, it amounts to more than the California gold production of ten years ago, when the all-time low for California was $8,500,000.

In Venezuela a proper exploitation of the gold fields which would make profitable the mining of the low-grade ore might bring the production to $50,000,000 a year, as it was in the California rush of 1856.

# CHAPTER XII

## *Pearls of Margarita*

IN COUNTING VENEZUELA'S BLESSINGS, one should not forget Margarita. It is the most important of some two dozen little Caribbean islands under the Venezuelan control.

With La Tortuga, Cubagua and Coche, it is a state with a capital at La Asunción. The group is called the state of Nueva Esparta.

The state has a population of some seventy thousand. The basic stock is of half-caste Quayqueri Indians, but the population has now become liberally mixed with Spanish blood. When you get away from the seashore, where there is still left a suggestion of the Africans, who arrived in slavery days, there are very few negroid evidences.

The island of Margarita has about four hundred square miles of territory, and lies less than twenty miles distant from the coast of Venezuela. Its history runs back to Christopher Columbus, who discovered it. Pirates who "sailed the Spanish Main and robbed the ships of Spain" used the island as a retreat and left it rich in the mythology of buried treasure.

The first topic any old-timer of Margarita takes up with you will relate to the carryings-on of these old buccaneers. You will even be told that descendants of various famous sea robbers are now diving for pearls at the waters of Pampatar and Porlamar, which are important pearl banks of Margarita.

For the richest buried treasure of Margarita and this group of islands, now and always, is hidden in oyster shells. In the early centuries of Spanish dominion, the pearl industry of this region was world famous. Queen Isabella wore a string of Venezuelan pearls. The citizens of Margarita will tell you that the most famous of the Queen's jewels came from Venezuela. There is history to support the local traditions. It is entirely possible that the value of the pearls which Spaniards have reclaimed from Margarita during the centuries is greater than the value of all the crown jewels with which Isabella financed the voyages of Columbus.

Certainly the pearls of Margarita were treasured in the courts of Europe, and were long regarded as among the finest pearls found anywhere. Philip II, so history says, owned a Margarita pearl of 250 carats. The chance that pearls of great price may at any time be found is what has kept the divers of Margarita at their toilsome work throughout the ages.

The government has taken over the regulation of the

pearl industry. In the interest of oyster-pearl conserva-
tion, it has established that there shall be an open season
on pearl diving once every three years, from June to
October, when everybody may dive for pearls. The industry is organized for concentrated activity during
those months.

Boats grouped in fleets of from sixty to seventy, with
ten divers for each boat, start at midnight of the opening day for the oyster banks. In the last open season
there were something like six hundred of these boats.
They arrive at sunrise, a signal gun is fired, and the
diving commences. A stone weighing about forty
pounds is attached to the cord by which the diver is let
down. Divers work in pairs, one man diving while the
other watches the signal cord, drawing up the sinkstone
first, then hauling up the baskets of oysters, and finally
raising the diver himself.

On an average, the divers remain under water from
fifty to ninety seconds, although exceptional instances
are cited where men have remained below as long as
six minutes.

For equilibrium upon the bottom of the sea, the diver
must use his toes. He arms himself with an iron spike
against the sharks and other fish which infest the Indian
waters. Indian divers seldom descend without incanta-
tions of snake charmers, one of whom accompanies the
boat, while others remain on shore.

Supernatural emotions seem to attach themselves to
the pearl business. Deity is taken into partnership in the

enterprise. When the season opens, even educated men go about saying, "May God grant" or there will be some precious pearls found "if God wills it so." When a Venezuelan is looking for a pearl as a gift to a friend, he says, "God grant that it may be worthy."

While head diving by native Indians remains the largest expression of the service, there have been frequent efforts to employ diving equipment.

The pearl comes from an oyster that has been irritated. When a diver looks for a likely oyster, he keeps his eyes open for those shells which are irregular in shape, stunted in growth, or disfigured in development. Shells that have been honeycombed by boring parasites are the most likely to yield pearls. When a pearl oyster is attacked by a boring parasite, the mollusk protects itself by depositing nacreous matter at the point of invasion, thus forming a hollow body of irregular shape, known as a "blister pearl."

The oysters yielding the best pearls are about four years of age.

Margarita is now talking about the destructive competition of the Japanese, who have invented a method of applying artificial wounds to oysters. Long ago the Chinese discovered that river mussels could be induced to yield pearls by inserting into them foreign bodies to form matrices for the deposit of pearl matter. The Japanese took advantage of the Chinese experiments, and now from the Japanese-controlled oyster beds come pearls that seem to match those of natural growth and cannot be distinguished except by scientific inspection. Thus they created what is known as a "culture pearl." The success of this artifice has become so great that it is diminishing the natural-pearl industry.

The known results of a fishing season for pearls run into a good many thousand bolivars, and the unknown results probably run high. Some remarkably fine pearls have been discovered in recent years. I was told of one from last year's take which sold for forty thousand bolivars. As a general thing, under the present situation, the pearls sell at from one and a half bolivars a carat up, according to their perfection and translucence.

Complete records as to the wealth of the pearl take are not ascertainable. Pearl fishing has always been rather a shifty business. If an individual diver finds a great pearl, he doesn't brag about it. He knows he can get a better price by going quietly over to Curaçao and selling it than by reporting it to the Venezuelan government. Smuggling is notorious in the Caribbean. The islanders from Margarita who cross over to Curaçao and trade in that free market smuggle their purchases back, just as they smuggle their pearls over to Curaçao.

It is impossible to compute the amount of pearls from the various oyster banks that might find their way into the hands of dealers of Curaçao. There is something about the very nature of the pearl industry which encourages stealth. While the government has declared a closed season on diving, there is generally somebody diving for pearls without the knowledge and consent of the government.

During the triennial open season the pearl dealers of the world come to Margarita to make inventory of the offerings. I was surprised to learn that the best-known traders were from Turkey, although the Paris, German and New York agents all find their way to this little harbor when the diving season is on.

The pearl industry does not constitute the entire wealth of this group of islands. The accumulated oyster shells provide a source of raw material from which factories make buttons the world over. The materials also contribute to the tortoise-shell industry, which gladdens the tourist by giving him an opportunity to carry home genuine tortoise-shell souvenirs.

Another important source of wealth is magnesia, which occurs in thick veins. The deposit lies in soft decomposed formation where it can be easily handled by steam shovels or other mechanical equipment. The silicate deposits of this island have been characterized as providing the highest grade of magnesia yet discovered.

There is a generous provision of nature in all the tropical plants.

The moriche palm, which abounds here and in various parts of Venezuela, is a general utility. From one part of it the native gets food; from another he makes a hat, fashions a basket, or forms a hammock. The spreading leaves he uses to provide a roof for his home, and from the body of the tree he fashions his canoe.

The oil of coconuts was once an exportable commodity, but has fallen a victim to modern science. With the largest oil refineries in the world located in this part of the Caribbean, coconut oil has gone to join the other unguents and illuminants that surrendered to the mass creation of petroleum "by-products."

# CHAPTER XIII

## *Tariff and Prices*

---

In EVERY COUNTRY the cost of living fluctuates somewhat with the economic pulse. In brisk times when money is plentiful, prices respond to an upward trend. In boom days the merchant, sensitive to the law of supply and demand, builds up the profit items in his stock account. He must be alive to the fact that it costs more to do business in good times than in bad times; the advancing problem of replacement is always warning him to keep on the safety side of the ledger.

In Venezuela today all the factors that make sensitive and jumpy the cost of living are in action.

At first you cannot realize the genesis of this boom. There are no sensational developments in the oil business, which has already placed the government beyond want, and which enriches its solvency by a constant increase in production. There have been no new discoveries of gold or precious metals.

The abnormal rush is due to the sudden lavish ex-

penditures by the government. Venezuela, in exerting
herself to spend over a billion bolivars on public works
in three years, has put a halo about the thing men call
"government." It would have been just as impossible in
the onrushing life of this spending program in Venezuela to cut down the prices of living as it would be to
regulate prices in the stampede of a new oil town or a
new gold field.

There is a shortage of labor. Wages are higher than
they are in any other country in South America—in
fact, common wages are higher than they are in the oil
fields in the United States, and top wages are fully
equal.

The essence of the boom is in the dreams and spirit
of government itself. The leaders are devoting their
whole thought and their resources to the curing of
everything which needs curing in Venezuela, so far as
it is curable.

A sort of social heaven has come down to earth, and
it has brought along the high prices that are inevitable.

The first thing the citizen who pays the high cost of
living tells you about is the Venezuelan tariff. This
seems to be an ancient evil, established probably when a
tariff for revenue was more important than it has been
since the advancing production of petroleum has made
easier the problem of governmental revenues.

The absurdity of a high protective tariff in a country
that is not producing any competitive article that
needed protection apparently had not occurred to the

government of Venezuela. So they kept on with probably the highest tariff wall in the world.

Americans who talked to me about the high cost of living are under a handicap peculiar to themselves. They discovered when they bought their exchange that a 59-cent United States dollar, which they had never known before, bought only 3.19 gold-standard bolivars. Before we devalued it, the United States dollar bought from five to seven bolivars. So the American in Venezuela who lives on dollars starts out with a new experience in his life; a realization that the United States dollar, while technically still a gold-standard expression of value at home, is a deflated piece of money, not good for one hundred cents in a land like Venezuela which has stuck to the old gold standard. This situation was further aggravated by additional increases in the tariff.

Naturally, the high-priced bolivar of Venezuela should produce a cheap price on the imported goods which Venezuela uses, but it doesn't. The height of the tariff wall more than overcomes the height of the dollar, after which must be taken into consideration the long bill of transportation.

There is no way of arriving at a general comparative basis on items, since custom duties are levied almost entirely on a specific basis. A broad guess would be that the tariff averages over 60 per cent ad valorem. In many of the most useful articles imported, it is 100 per cent ad valorem. In automobiles it is generally 100 per cent.

Mass figures on dutiable imports and customs are revealing.

In 1937 the dutiable imports amounted in value to 178,715,000 bolivars. The customs revenue upon this importation was 133,825,000 bolivars, being 74½ per cent tax on the entire importation of dutiable imports into the country. The estimate of import duties for 1939 is set at 113,000,000 bolivars. For 1938 the oil royalties amounted to 253,328,830.80 bolivars. In addition, in various taxes the oil companies paid Venezuela in 1938 96,505,715.93 bolivars. For 1939 they were somewhat in advance of this.

Boots and shoes cost twice as much in Venezuela as they do in Puerto Rico. A suit of clothes which sells for $18 in Puerto Rico sells for $60 in Venezuela. An Allis Chalmers tractor which sells for $1,000 in the United States sells for $1,800 here.

A correct list of food prices from Venezuelan grocery stores, which has been carefully checked, is revealing. In Caracas, for example, eggs cost the consumer 95 cents a dozen; potatoes, 32 cents a pound; beef costs 44 cents a pound. These are all domestic products. Bread made from imported flour costs 32 cents a pound, and imported flour itself costs 13 cents a pound. Canned peas cost 48 cents per can imported; a native chicken costs $1.90; a head of cabbage raised in a Venezuelan garden costs 40 cents, and a pound of butter made in a Venezuelan dairy costs $1.22.

We are talking in dollars, not bolivars.

The significant fact is that the prices for domestic products are fully as high as those paid for imported commodities, sometimes higher. A pound of salt costs 60 cents, although it is produced in Venezuela. A quart of fresh Venezuelan milk costs 24 cents, but you can get a can of powdered milk from the United States, capable of making several quarts, for 72 cents. Rice, which is raised in some abundance in Venezuela, costs 13 cents per pound; an 8-cent can of Campbell's soup costs 40 cents.

I was somewhat disturbed to hear discussion of "price fixing" by government bureaus in an effort to keep down the cost of living. If they want to know why such a course, though enormously expensive to the tax-payer, is doomed to failure, they can get all the facts quickly by examining our record in the United States in this field. And they can learn from our record too that if production goes up prices will go down, provided tariff duties do not interfere.

With orange orchards growing everywhere, Venezuelan consumers pay exorbitant prices for canned fruit juices. Canned orange juice, in a land of oranges, is easier to buy than the native fruit.

Venezuelans import dried fruits to a land which abounds with tropical fruits of every variety. They grow the best cocoa in the world, but import their chocolate bars over a high tariff wall.

With sugar cane willing to grow wild without much cultivation, they give you, for the purpose of sweetening your lemonade, a syrup made in the United States.

So far as I was able to determine, there was not a single industry in Venezuela that has been protected by the tariff. In this connection it is comforting to remember that there is now going on in Venezuela a movement to reduce customs tariffs. It is proposed, with much probability that the scheme will be accepted, to put a flat reduction on all tariff duties that now affect the high price of living.

The duty on imported steel furniture, for example, is very heavy, amounting to at least 100 per cent.

A Venezuelan factory assembles an inferior product from entirely imported materials and sells it at unbelievably high prices. In an article like this, foreign exporters cannot compete in this market. The only business they get on household equipment is from the government, which buys for its new hospitals and schools great quantities of equipment made in the United States.

Around Venezuela are beautiful mahogany forests, as well as red cedars, but by the time enough wood is cut and reaches the trade, it costs $170 per thousand, which is about what white pine imported from the United States costs. The immediate problem principally is labor. With the easy locations of forests, transportation would make it possible to assemble these mahogany trees at lumber mills, if there were lumber mills.

The greatest drawback in Venezuela as yet is the lack of initiative on the part of the people, to the detriment of agriculture and other industrial developments.

There is growing up a very definite and intelligent protest on the part of various writers, both in the press and magazines, against the high tariff wall. The attention of the leadership of Venezuela is being called sharply to the realization that a tariff wall like this is not justified by any of the conditions in Venezuela.

I was glad to note in one of President Lopez Contreras' messages his reference to this problem. I heard it discussed many times by government leaders. I have faith that they will arrive at a just solution of a condition obviously out of setting in a land that is doing so many fine things for the comfort and progress of its people.

With the strengthening of the population through the drive for better conditions now being made all along the line, it is to be hoped that a new initiative will come to the private capital of Venezuela, which has been made timid by the government's spending program. Either tapering off of government expenditures, or more expenditures allocated to activities which would increase the productive enterprise of the nation and its people, might serve effectively in stimulating Venezuelan capital to undertake to develop the admirable resources of the country for the profit of the general public, as well as for itself. Venezuelan capital, which grows in strength, will not remain content to let the outside money do all the developing in a land where the diversified opportunities should be tempting to the citizen.

## CHAPTER XIV

# *A Nation Busy at Public Works*

---

DURING 1938–39, 133 government buildings, erected or remodeled, have seen a saving of as high as 40 per cent on the unit cost. Eager young engineers are enthusiastic, not only over the quality of work but the speed of it, whether done under contract or by direct government operation.

The shovel leaner is doubtless here, as everywhere, but he isn't organized as yet. Some justification and latitude is given him by the prevalency of the hookworm, but he has no political license to lean. The principal labor problem is in the shortage of laborers.

The new constructive example of the government has affected, somewhat, the contractors on private work. Everyone is getting a sort of civic religion.

The building boom has been growing steadily. New additions spring up everywhere. In any substantial city you are shown some amazing developments, generally in residential property.

In some instances, such as that at Maracay, where the Gómez ranch has been broken up into twelve-acre parcels for individual small farms, good houses are being built with the credit aid of the Agricultural and Cattle Bank.

In Puerto Cabello, for example, where many hundreds of houses have been built for the workers on the new wharfs, docks and port activities, the houses have been erected with the credit aid of the Labor Bank.

The credit assistance which has been given both by the Agriculture and Cattle Bank and by the Labor Bank, which are two institutions under one administration, has been helpful. The agricultural and cattle program, which has made distinctive advance, has not, of course, shown the progress as that under the Labor Bank, because the very demand for workers has reduced the attention to agriculture.

No money has been spent on so-called agrarian aids to control croppage. The agricultural problem in Venezuela is not that of decreasing production; on the contrary it is the problem of increasing production. About the only agrarian artifice established is in a plan to subsidize certain agricultural productions which have suffered under the protective tariff wall of the Republic or the high value of its money.

The Labor Bank, however, has found plenty to do because of the rapid increase in the employment of labor in communities where housings have been inadequate. The new law requiring suitable housings for

workmen, following lines already inaugurated by the
oil companies, is spreading through the other large industries of the nation. In fact, the housing program is
going forward at a tempo which is fairly hectic.

The present law limits the loan on any house to
12,000 bolivars, which would be about 3,800 United
States dollars. The bank is authorized to sell its houses,
to rent them, or to lease them with option to buy. The
bank may charge interest rates of from 4 to 6 per cent—
the rate of amortization is 3 per cent. The dealer has a
right to make larger payments for amortization. In case
of a lease with option to buy, the monthly rent is fixed
at one half of one per cent of the cash price of the
house.

When the amounts paid on the account, either by
rental or capital payment or by both, equal one half the
value of the house, the tenant has a right to acquire it by
purchase, with a mortgage on the balance due.

In Caracas, where the rate of building is estimated at
three and a half houses a day, the Labor Bank has
built a great many houses, but the private real-estate
investors have been responsible for even a larger number.

The government work at Puerto Cabello has made
it one of the most important ports in the Caribbean.
Work on the new warehouses, wharfs, dry docks and
workers' colonies has been going on for over a year.
The project was recently dedicated by President Lopez
Contreras on a special visit made for that purpose.

Practically every modern feature of equipment I have ever seen in any port around the world has turned up to become a part of this ambitious effort of Venezuela to leave nothing unbought which might contribute to the successful activity of a modern port. The workers' cottages, hundreds of them, in a pleasing addition set apart from the old town, constitute in reality a modern village of small but thoroughly up-to-date houses. I do not believe that in all the world there is another dock-walloper village in its class.

I was comforted, when I visited the port, at the array of United States machinery which a Grace liner had just deposited at the new docks. Dodge trucks, Ford tractors, station wagons, caterpillar tractors, passenger automobiles of several United States makes, iron pipes, barbed wire, building boards, fabricated houses, plumbing supplies, sawmills and road machinery had taken possession of the ample docks. It was a homelike collection of United States commodities. There were a few pieces of German machinery and one contribution from an English factory, but the remainder bore the United States brand.

For several years the petroleum companies have maintained technical schools, devoting great attention to teaching the young Venezuelans engineering, accountancy, geology, administration, office management, stenography and English. They have taught them how to be drillers, road graders, carpenters, masons, plumbers, welders, tractor drivers and mechanics. Now the government, with its tremendously emphasized program of public works, is absorbing this trained personnel of the oil companies faster than the oil companies can prepare it for themselves, thus not only creating a shortage of labor but handicapping the one industry which is training Venezuelans to become better workmen.

One practical effort to relieve the pressure in technical activities in Venezuela has been the establishment of an Institute of Geology. In a land where 80 per cent of the exports are extracted directly from the ground, geology becomes of great educational importance. Today there is going on all over Venezuela a scientific search for subsurface riches. In contemplating the possible exhaustion of oil, which the most advanced geologists tell me is not likely to come about for some time, there is a new enthusiasm about the possible minerals which have not already been explored. It is known that there are deposits of magnesite, phosphates, asbestos, gold, even diamonds, and a large iron deposit, the latter now under lease to the Bethlehem Steel Company. Therefore the announcement of a practical Institute of Geology to give proficient courses to geologists who can be used, not only directly in economic geology but in soil studies, erosion control, engineering projects, water-supply projects and other undertakings, was of first importance.

The institute is now running under the technical direction of Professor N. B. Knox, a mining geologist from the Stanford University class-of 1931. There are seven members of the faculty: two American, two German, one French and two Venezuelan, each with his own separate laboratory.

While the institute is small, its equipment and faculty give it a superior standing. The methods of instruction and examination are something new in Venezuelan education. Examinations of the objective type are given monthly, followed by final examinations at the end of the semester. Major emphasis is placed on laboratory work and practical application of the subjects studied.

The purpose of the institute is to give a full four years' course leading to a degree, which should be the equivalent of a United States or English bachelor's degree in geology. English is the only foreign language taught there. The rest of the time is taken up by the practical studies of the geological sciences and the sciences upon which these are based.

A splendidly stocked library gives an opportunity for a broader cultural interest, and the character of the faculty justifies the feeling that, in addition to their training in geology, the students will acquire a broad culture.

The tuition is free, but no student is allowed to enter until he has received a "bachillerato," which corresponds to the English higher-school certificate and the United States junior-college certificate. After receiving this certificate the student must still pass a competitive entrance examination.

Foreign students are admitted. Each class starts with

only twenty-four students, a new class being admitted every two years.

Added encouragement is given by six fellowships for students from the following nations: Cuba, Mexico, Peru, Colombia, Panama and Brazil, the incumbents for these fellowships to be named by the ministers of these countries to Venezuela.

The oil companies operating in Venezuela have aided the institute by setting up eight scholarships for Venezuelan students. These scholarships allow a student living expenses during the four years of his course and offer him opportunity to do practical field work with the companies during vacation.

There is today every sort of rush for more geologists. The oil companies are carrying on large explorations all over Venezuela, having recently developed important production in the central and eastern part of the country. The government is exploring the Grand Savannah and other great plains, making a general geological survey to determine the mineral content of the subsoil, as well as agricultural possibilities. In addition there is the new water program which is calling for geological engineers to aid in the drilling of wells for water supply. The problem of a job for a young citizen does not present itself in Venezuela.

# CHAPTER XV

## *Sanitation and Hospitalization*

---

THE BEGINNING OF BETTER DAYS to a people plagued with tropical maladies which make sick the body and morbid the mind is in modern sanitation. Therefore, when I was told that a practical sanitary unit for free clinics, visiting nurses, motorized first aid and all the gadgets that go with the latest expression of municipal sanitary service had been opened, I went with keen interest to look over the new institution.

Social service had made only a fair start before Lopez Contreras' day, whereas now new sanitary units are being established almost simultaneously in all the populous territories of Venezuela. There is for them no pioneer period, with its makeshifts, waiting for funds for particular needs or holding public entertainments to whip the popular sentiment so that the work may prosper under growing public opinion.

The first unit of what is bound to be an outstanding model to the whole tropical world was established in an old house where Simón Bolívar lived as a boy and studied with his tutors. It has been enlarged and glorified, and it shines like a new automobile. Into it has been brought every type of equipment known to modern science. It is something more than a sanitary unit, being amongst other things a sort of junior hospital for infants and expectant mothers.

There is a school of instruction for parents, with a manual-training department where they are taught to make baby beds of boxes and baskets, baby clothes out of cheap materials, household furniture out of waste lumber. Mothers are given lessons in housekeeping, taught how to clean utensils and how to make the best use of soap and water. They are also taught how to bathe their babies. We in the United States initiated similar activities about one generation ago, and Venezuela, which had been waiting four hundred years for this lesson, is not far behind us.

A giant chart hangs on the wall of the reception room with the names of many mothers who are enrolled as patrons of the clinic. Beside some of the names is placed a gold peg, beside others a green peg, others red, and amongst the last a black peg. These symbols denote the response of the mothers to the teaching of child care, housekeeping and the general observance of the lessons of health and sanitation. A dozen visiting nurses, each charged with the task of looking after 120 families, bring in reports from the homes and make up the grades of these contestant mothers. Mothers with gold symbols in front of their names get first prize; the green tag gets second prize; the red one draws further help and encouragement, and the black one draws a close investigation to discover what there is about these mothers that make them unresponsive to the work of health reform. This new type of regimentation is peculiarly advanced in a land which has had no health direction.

There is a children's clinic to which are sent all school children who have been examined by the visiting nurses in the schools and found to be in need of attention. If they need medical or hospital treatment and are without funds, they go to the free new children's hospital, recently completed, with over three hundred beds, where they get immediate care. If they happen to be children of well-to-do parents, they are sent to the particular doctor who is employed by that family and whose duty it is to give immediate attention to the diagnosis of the government clinic.

The clinic serves pasteurized milk and looks after the children's diet in a large way.

In this first unit there are eight doctors and eight nurses to care for the one hundred children a day who come for examination.

Modern trucks, which are a cross between an ambulance and a first-aid dressing station, wait to carry visiting nurses to emergency cases.

The building is supplied with operating rooms, equipped with the largest instruments of radiology, electrical surgery, a dental office with three chairs, X-ray appurtenances and every appliance known to high-priced dentistry the world around. Here the teeth of a people never before introduced to dentistry are subject to attention. While provision is made particularly for children, the parents get some consideration, and the expert dentists—whom the state employs to go as far as they like—were busy providing amalgam fillings and doing such other things as dentists find to do on teeth from the cradle to the grave.

An emergency maternity ward takes care of the immediate necessity of those who have not yet gone to the maternity hospital.

The director of the new unit is only twenty-six years of age, but is attracting attention by the capability with which he is administering this new movement in public health. He is a native Venezuelan of Indian parentage, who was graduated from Johns Hopkins, where he had been sent as a government student. There are now in Johns Hopkins eight government students being taught public health service.

While the sanitary units established to deal with general community healths are hopeful beyond any ordinary expectation in the progress they are making in health matters in Venezuela, the most impressive revelation is their hospitalization. When someone told me of the seven new hospitals and sanatoriums that had been created in Caracas alone as the result of the new Three Year Plan, I was skeptical. "Created on paper?" I asked, with the slightly raised inflection which produces irritation.

I paid for my doubts. Challenged immediately to visit each one of these new institutions in company with medical experts, I spent the better part of seven days visiting them, in order to make a thorough job of it. I must have traveled over one hundred acres of tiled floors, climbed miles of stairways, been shoved into innumerable caverns of radiological darkness, and made to peep into the most amazing operating rooms I have ever seen.

The institutions were all new, and therefore time's latest offspring. With the exception of one which was to be opened in two months, they were finished and seemed incredibly busy.

I saw such convincing exhibitions of what had been done in from a year and a half to two years that I sat me down and gasped in frank amazement that new hospitalization providing something like three thousand beds had been created during that period for specialized and general purposes, the services of all of them being a free gift to people who could not pay.

We visited the new maternity hospital, which was housed in a modern fireproof, air-conditioned building, four stories high, built with a patio in the center, giving the wards light from all sides. I have not seen a more convincing institution. This most modern thing in Caracas is the outgrowth of an original conference for mothers held by Governor Mabelli, the able head of the Federal District. He has not only a great sympathy for all people but a loving enthusiasm for children. In studying his plans for various municipal improvements, he had solicited the opinions of many people who had specialized in that form of welfare work. He created Mothers' Day and Sons' Day in Venezuela. He had co-operation in his social planning with Katharine Lenroot, of Washington, who had visited Venezuela to give him the benefit of her experience and studies.

The governor, now a middle-aged man, for fifteen years of his life had been a political prisoner. Lopez Contreras, who knew of his general abilities and his humanitarian ideals, released him and gave him the governorship of the Federal District, which corresponds somewhat to our District of Columbia.

The maternity hospital has 160 beds and an installation that contains every perfection of modern thought, from the radio-equipped ambulances that stand waiting for emergency calls in the basement corridor to the automatically controlled American elevators which take the patients to the wards. As I went through the place, I kept noticing that the operating rooms and laboratories were supplied with radiological, electric and X-ray mechanisms from the United States. Most of the kitchen and laundry equipment came from Germany. The maternity hospital has given to the poorest women in Venezuela, free of charge, an attention to their maternity needs mechanistically more up to date and elaborate than the rich enjoy in the several excellent private clinics of the city.

As I went through the various wards where the beds

were occupied by scores of mothers waiting their labors, I asked what they did with the babies. A doctor took me in an elevator to a corner on the top floor. I hadn't heard the cry of a baby in the whole busy institution, where new babies were the order of the day. When we entered a private corridor, the doctor went to a cabinet, brought me a gauze mask for my nose and mouth, then, putting on his mask, he rapped on the mahogany door of a closed room. It opened, and immediately I was in a room full of tiny beds, and a steady wail was going up from over one hundred babies who were giving their lungs the modern freedom to cry as loudly and long as they wished. The room was soundproof, scientifically treated with modern air conditioning, and the two nurses who presided over the room looked as proud as though they had done the whole thing themselves.

Twenty per cent of the mothers in the maternity hospital are afflicted with syphilis, and twenty-two per cent of their babies die at birth. The problem of the amelioration of venereal disease in this tropical country at last has been attacked with an intelligent although a somewhat restraining treatment.

I learned also that a modern and effective clinic for the treatment of cancer has been established. The doctors have made no new discoveries, but they are up to the minute on the world program.

As I went through the basement of the maternity hospital, going out, there was some kind of trouble. A young Indian girl, acting as a student helper, had suffered a nervous breakdown and used a knife on a young doctor. The doctor had already bandaged the cut in his arm and was helping with utmost gentleness to calm the wild-eyed young girl, who had been placed between two policemen to be driven to the psychiatric hospital—also a new institution for mental cases. Three years ago, in all probability, she would have gone to a prison cell.

I visited next the new clinical hospital. A very beautiful new building, on a tall hill overlooking Caracas, it would be hailed as an impressive thing in any city. It is constructed on a special plan which takes into consideration the tropical needs. Long wings go out from a main structure with patios separating them, leaving room for a bit of landscaping and affording each ward and room an outside location with a pleasing prospect.

This hospital had just been completed. It is to be run as a clinical institution in connection with the university. It has 360 beds, laboratories galore, classrooms, operating rooms, and every known thing in radiology, electrical surgery and capacity for modern research and student demonstration. It has cost over a million bolivars ($332,000). The planner, architects and builders have beaten the speed of the medical educators who must administer the institution. The building is really ready ahead of time.

I was taken next to a receiving hospital for tubercular patients, which had just been finished on the site of an old folks' home, long abandoned. It stands in the heart of the city and offers free treatment. In its elaborate attention to tuberculosis cases, in which this hospital specializes, it has a modern department for adults separated from an equally important one for children. With vast pride my guides showed me equipment for examination of lungs under modern visual surgery, for the injection of air into a collapsed lung, and every known aid to every development of pulmonary treatment.

The patients are studied carefully for classification of their needs. This institution is to co-ordinate its work with that of the great antituberculosis sanatorium then nearing completion and capable of giving modern treatment to a thousand cases of tuberculosis infection in all stages.

The medicines of this clinic are free. An odd feature of its distribution of medicine is that on every bottle given out there is a bit of propaganda advertising the lotteries as an important adjunct of Venezuelan health! This is accounted for by the fact that hospitalization in Caracas in particular, and in Venezuela as a whole in some degree, is paid for out of profits of the national lotteries. Last year, for Caracas alone, the lottery yielded 6,151,859.80 bolivars. In addition to this, 958,309 bolivars were distributed under a special law to the hospitalization in the various states.

Most of the states of Venezuela have lotteries, but since the lottery at Caracas yields so much more than in any other part of Venezuela, a distribution is set aside for additional welfare services in communities outside of the Federal District.

By the time the medical men had shown me three great new hospitals, I asked anxiously if there were really four more. They told me that, including the psychiatric, which they had forgotten to mention, there were five more, if we counted the sanitary unit.

Of all the hospitals I visited, the most poignant spot was called Pabellon Infantil, a municipal sanatorium for tubercular children. There is an interesting story about its foundation. Ladis Lao Aponte was a sick Indian orphan about ten years old. He blacked boots when he was able, begged food when he was not too sick. He was a symbol of many parentless children who were equally helpless. When he became desperately ill, he didn't seem to fit into any of the limited categories for which government care was provided. He was picked up in the gutters in an advanced stage of tuberculosis. Caracas was just beginning to respond to the emotions of the new social program. So the health authorities carried this desolate lad out to an old house on an abandoned little farm in a quiet mountain valley. They fixed up rude shelters, gave him treatment and became interested in the rallying of his strength.

Something about his case stimulated an outburst of sympathetic interest, and in a short while other indigent children afflicted by tuberculosis were brought to this little pocket in the mountains. It developed in two years into a most efficient tubercular retreat. The old house was reconstructed and pavilions as well as closed wards were added. The little Indian lad seemed to possess some flame that spiritualized the movement, and all Venezuela watched it grow as an expression of public concern.

Now it is a singularly attractive institution, possessing an outdoor kindergarten and ground for the cultivation, by children who are able to work, of flowers and vegetables.

Like all of the other institutions of cure in Venezuela, it has now been furnished with every possible equipment for the treatment of these little patients, including doctors and resident nurses. But the first thing the medical men do when you enter the pavilion is to take you into a reception room and point to the picture of Ladis Lao Aponte, which has been placed upon the wall. They tell you of his value as the spiritual founder of the institution.

He died only a few months before my visit. They were never able to effect a cure of his pulmonary maladies, but they prolonged his life for nearly three years, and today they give him credit for the organization of this beautiful work which now has two hundred patients who receive every attention of the government.

The inspector general of the hospitalization in the Federal District, Dr Pedro Gonzales Rincones, one of the ablest of the medical fraternity in Venezuela and one of the enthusiasts responsible for the new hospitalization, wouldn't draw the curtain on my efforts until I had visited the old Vargas hospital. It was constructed over sixty years ago, with something like five hundred beds, and is now being rebuilt, a wing at a time, and equipped with every modern facility. It is going to be turned over to Venezuela as a free hospital.

No greater revolution in the spirit of the humanities has occurred than in the rebuilding of what they call the psychiatric hospital. This means in Venezuela the hospital for the insane. It, as well as its counterparts in most civilized countries until a few years ago, was the gloomiest manifestation of indifference and unconscious cruelty. Until recently the methods of caring for the insane in nearly all countries were born of seventeenth-century practice.

This vile old building was razed one old wing at a time and a new one built and furnished with scientific care, and modern features were copied from the outstanding institutions of psychiatry throughout the world.

The new structure has mammoth proportions—one wing for women is six hundred feet long. Workrooms for patients whose mental qualifications determine their eligibility are established all over the place. I visited one ward in which a great number of Singer sewing machines were giving employment to patients. Other patients were making shoes, clothes, rude furniture out of mahogany cut from near-by trees.

The superintendent showed me with deep satisfaction

the psychiatric library in which every important book on mental diseases is available for the use of the staff doctors.

The institution's system of selling the handiwork of the patient and turning part of his money to a savings account, giving him part for spending money, was gone into at an enthusiastic length. It wasn't new to one acquainted with methods at home, but it was new in Venezuela, as new as the idea of seeking a permanent cure for mental cases in a public institution.

There was an interesting activity which I had never before heard of in connection with a hospital for the insane. Out of its ample kitchens the institution was supplying a near-by rural school for boys with cooked food and pure milk. The boys were furnishing vegetables from their gardens to the kitchen of the hospital. It was a delightful picture of human co-operation.

In connection with this hospital for the insane, in a separate building, was an elaborate home for the nurses. An entirely modern building, it gave first-class accommodations for thirty or forty nurses. Each nurse had her own room; each room a private bath. Dining rooms, recreation rooms, library all contributed to the exclusive atmosphere. When I commented upon the fact that nurses in insane asylums were generally attendants whose nursing duties were somewhat incidental, the hospital authorities explained to me that efforts were being made to build up the nursing morale in Venezuela, where for centuries the nurse had been rated as a servant. The hope was to make nursing an attractive and honored profession.

In some respects the most remarkable hospitalization I have ever seen is the Antituberculosis Sanatorium. It is a model for institutions of similar character to be built in other parts of the nation. One at Mérida, in the Andean region, was already under construction.

The site of the antituberculosis hospital is about a half-dozen miles from Caracas, in a secluded mountain valley which provides a veritable spot of climate. The mountains moderate the breezes, and the altitude, which is slightly over three thousand feet, provides a salubrious temperature.

The institution spreads over acres of ground; in some parts—for the closed wards—it is two stories high. Outside are pavilions for open-air treatment, and between all these pavilions are attractive parkings in which flowers and shrubberies are being planted.

The project is costing over 6,000,000 bolivars. The experts who co-operated in its planning have brought from the wide world every provision for the effective treatment of pulmonary troubles. It will care for over one thousand patients.

Upon the brow of taller ground, looking down upon the spreading sanatorium, are two handsome buildings —one to house the doctors of the hospital and the other the nurses. They are significant of the plan to make a finished job of every institution at the time of construction. In most countries, the finishing touches of the service, such as the nurses' home, the doctors' residence and the other refinements of a complete job, have to wait for a better hour. Here the service knows no pioneer period of waiting for anything.

It may seem that I have dwelt too much upon the subject of Venezuelan hospitals. As a matter of fact, nothing is so convincing of the new day in Venezuela as this hospitalization. For a good many years everything written about Venezuela has emphasized the need of more medical attention. The great plagues of the country, those which cause the highest mortality and undermine the health and stamina of the people in general, are the same that are found everywhere in tropical America—malaria, syphilis, intestinal parasites, especially hookworm, so prevalent in southern United States, tropical dysentery, and in the valleys the dread disease of schistosomiasis.

On reading the statistics of causes of death in the whole country, you do not get the true picture, for with the exception of malaria, very few cases are attributed to the other diseases mentioned, because these diseases seldom terminate fatally. They so weaken the whole organism that the individual falls prey to any intercurrent disease and dies for lack of normal defensive powers.

The tremendous efforts now being given to hospitalization and medicine merely exhibit the depth of realization that Venezuela is a country whose people must be brought to a proper condition of good health.

Therefore, the establishment of hospitalization, of medical training, of nurses' training, and general interest all along the line are a reflection of the fact that when the President put sanitation and hospitalization as one of the great needs of the day, he marked it as a first need.

I thought it would be valuable to have an estimate of the health situation in Venezuela by a doctor who is not an employee of the government staff. I asked Dr E. P. de Bellard, one of the successful practitioners of Caracas, to give me a résumé of the subject. Dr de Bellard has had many years of practice in tropical climates. He came to Caracas twenty years ago from New Orleans, a graduate of Tulane University; he has built a successful modern clinic of his own and is recognized as an outstanding medical man in Venezuela. The following statement from him, therefore, possesses a certain disinterestedness of a private practitioner:

"The fight against tropical maladies presents very great and serious problems in so large a country so thinly populated. Their eradication is theoretically but not practically possible. The impressive and successful sanitation of the Canal Zone by General Gorgas is as child's play compared with the Venezuelan problem. It would involve an effort and an expenditure far above the resources of even as rich a country as Venezuela.

Only local measures are at present within the scope of possibilities, and the government of General Lopez Contreras is attacking the problem with energy and as much success as can possibly be expected. What is being accomplished can best be appreciated by the constant decline in infant mortality in the Federal District, where it has declined from 150 per thousand live births per annum four years ago to 93 per thousand, which is comparable with the best showing of any city on the American continent south of the United States. And this death rate is declining every year.

"What has been accomplished in social service in the short time of the Lopez Contreras' regime is astonishing: public dispensaries, magnificent hospitals, anti-venereal clinics, tuberculosis sanatoriums, emergency stations, everything that may contribute to the health and well-being of the masses, and the prevention and treatment of disease has been created overnight, you might say. And the staffs in charge of the different services are competent, well prepared and energetic.

"With the creation of so many hospitals and dispensaries and the tremendous expansion of the social-service organizations suddenly demanding a large number of nurses, an acute situation has arisen in connection with the shortage of qualified nurses which has not yet been solved. It takes three years to train a nurse, and the newly organized schools of nurses will eventually solve the problem. But it will take time. At present it is very difficult to get a competent nurse to take care of a private patient; the social-service organizations have absorbed most of them, and at salaries with which the private clinics cannot compete. The health movement as initiated by General Lopez Contreras found Venezuela unprepared. The nursing profession, as we know it in the States, did not exist and had to be created. The demure, well-bred, educated Venezuelan young lady would not think of studying to be a nurse; it was almost disgraceful. It was the girl of the servant class, with scant education and very little training, who put on a white dress and did her best to minister to the sick.

"A tribute of admiration should here be paid to Miss Ysabel Helena Gómez Velutini, a brilliant girl, highly trained and endowed with exceptional abilities, for raising the nursing profession to its present honorable and competent standard. She has been for years a fine example, a symbol and an inspiration, and has blazed the trail for many another fine girl to embrace the most useful and exacting profession to which a woman can devote her life and energies. Miss Gómez has been indeed the Florence Nightingale of Venezuela.

"Another acute problem, indeed a grim and sad reality, is the great shortage of physicians in the interior remote places where their services are most needed. On the other hand, there is a superabundance of doctors and specialists in the capital. All recent graduates aspire to settle in Caracas, with the result that the rest of the country is insufficiently covered. However, the government is doing its best to remedy this distressing situation by offering tempting salaries and freedom to practice medicine to physicians willing to settle in the country districts.

"The task of creating a service of visiting nurses is now being attempted, but meets with the difficulty of the shortage of nurses. As the schools of nurses turn out new professionals, this branch of the social service will improve. The only immediate solution would be the importation of a number of Spanish-speaking nurses.

"The dental and pharmaceutical professions are well organized, and there is an efficient dental clinic in every hospital."

I should add, however, that the government is already preparing to deal in a very effective way with the shortage of country doctors. At the Ministry of Health I was told they are going to require of all medical graduates two years of practice in country work—preferably in their home communities, if these lack doctors.

Venezuela, in common with other South American countries, has received valuable aid from the Rockefeller Foundation in the battle with poor health conditions. The gifts of the Foundation to Venezuela have no connection with the extensive activities of the Standard Oil Company, nor has there ever been any link in the work of the two institutions there.

The first assistance from the Rockefeller Foundation

was given to Venezuela in 1916 during a severe yellow-fever epidemic. When the World War conditions suspended the activities of the Rockefeller Foundation, the Gómez government, making use of the surveys of the Foundation, undertook for itself the yellow-fever control.

Seven years later, when it was feared that infection would spread through Maracaibo from Colombia, the International Health Board (now called the International Health Division) of the Foundation again entered the field. They made a survey of the situation and appropriated $10,000 for the eradication of the disease. The following year, when the need of another survey became apparent, an appropriation of $5,000 was granted, in addition to a previously appropriated sum of $75,000 in Colombia.

Dr Henry Hanson and Major L. H. Dunn, members of the Board, reported in 1925 that no yellow fever had been evident in Venezuela for some months.

At that time the attention of the country was turning to public health. Dr W. A. Sawyer, now director of the International Health Division, went to Venezuela to work out a program of co-operation with the government. On the recommendation of Dr Sawyer the International Health Board agreed to lend the services of a sanitary engineer, a member of the Board's staff, and to grant fellowships for the training of public-health personnel.

Beneficial results followed the efforts of these experienced members of the International Health Board. The work had the support of the Venezuelan government.

By 1936 the Contreras administration was inaugurating its health program. They were undertaking a program of rural sanitation, endeavoring to build up an Institute of Hygiene and to improve water supplies and sewage disposal. Dr Enrique Tejera, then Minister of Public Health, requested the aid of the International Health Division of the Rockefeller Foundation. Representatives of the Division visited Venezuela that year and reported that the country needed both engineering personnel and equipment in order to fulfill its responsibilities under a new law which had created a Malaria Commission. Arrangements were made by the Division for seven engineers and two physicians to visit drainage and sanitation work in Panama and Costa Rica at the government's expense.

Perhaps the most significant part of the assistance by the International Health Division has been the granting of fellowships for the training of Venezuelan professional personnel in the United States. Fellowship training was given to a sanitary engineer in 1929–30. A fellowship in public-health administration was granted in 1933. Since 1936, under a program in which emphasis is placed more definitely on the thorough training of experts, seven additional fellowships have been given for training at Johns Hopkins School of Hygiene and Public Health, Harvard School of Public Health, and the University of Toronto School of Nurs-

ing. At the same time, a number of Venezuelan government fellows have been assisted and their work super-
vised to some extent by the fellowship adviser of the
International Health Division of the Foundation.

# CHAPTER XVI

## *Solving the Problem of Pure Water*

---

It WOULD BE USELESS to establish sanitary units and build hospitals to improve the health of Venezuela if the present effort stopped at the accomplishment of this objective, great as it is.

In the tropics, the part which water plays in the transmission of diseases is far more important than has been recognized in the past. Water-supply engineers have developed the fact that the purification of all surface supplies by filtration and disinfection is absolutely essential. Even if the waters are practically clear and colorless, the many causes of pollution make necessary the severest sanitary inspection. Filtration plants are necessary because it has been discovered that chloridation is not sufficiently effective to safeguard against many of the water-borne diseases, such as typhoid fever and bacillary dysentery, also diseases caused by parasitic worms more common than in the temperate north.

In Caracas, the chief city of the nation, the old water

pipes and the pipes carrying the sewage had reached a state where both leaked. Running parallel with each other, it wasn't unusual for contents of the sewage pipes to invade the water pipes, with deadly results. The unsanitary conditions in other cities and good-sized towns were equally disturbing. Whether the water came from an unclean pipe line or was impounded from the surface, it was equally fatal to health.

Dr George C. Bunker, a competent sanitation engineer of the United States, a specialist on the subject of water supply, has been employed at the head of the amazing effort on foot to cleanse the waters of Venezuela.

Dr Bunker was engaged in November 1936 to act as adviser to the Minister of Public Works for the government relative to the entire subject of development and purification of water supplies. As the first step he installed a laboratory for chemical and bacteriological examinations.

He has spent a good many years in designing, studying and constructing various water supplies in Colombia and the Panama Canal Zone, all of them being subject to the strict sanitary specifications demanded for the work of this character in the United States.

You do not need to be told of the progress they are making in Caracas. Lines of workmen swarm everywhere in torn-up streets, hurrying forward the installation of pipes for water supply and for drainage.

The sewage section of Caracas, built by the adminis-

*A Venezuelan family.*

tration in one year, has gone forward at a speed which amounts to almost a mile a month, at a cost nearly 40 per cent under the unit estimate—a saving accomplished by the intense application with which the work has been pushed.

In seven cities of Venezuela I found the same rush proceeding. It takes your breath away to be shown the completed plans for seventy-one major water plants in seventy-one important cities of Venezuela and in thirteen towns of lesser importance, 20 per cent of which are well under way.

The status of the water works at the end of April 1939 was about as follows:

|  | Number | *Per Cent of Total Number* |
|---|---|---|
| Under study | 30 | 35.72 |
| Ready to start | 3 | 3.57 |
| Under construction | 37 | 44.05 |
| Work suspended temporarily | 2 | 2.38 |
| Completed | 12 | 14.28 |
|  | 84 | 100.00 |

At the present time it is the intention of the Ministry of Public Works to construct filtration plants of the rapid sand type in the following cities: Caracas, Maracaibo, Valencia, San Cristóbal, Mérida, Ciudad Bolívar, Valera, Puerto Cabello and Lagunillas. However, it is probable that filtration plants will have to be constructed in some of the other cities as the studies progress.

There is one small pressure filtration plant in operation to supply water to Turmero and Cagua (near Maracay).

The new modern water-supply system in Maracaibo will be the first to be completed in the group of the largest cities. It was expected that this system would be completed by January 1940. The system consists of sixteen deep wells, a water-treatment plant, with a capacity of 8,000,000 gallons per day, to remove iron and manganese, a 34-inch reinforced concrete pipe line approximately 14.5 kilometers long, a covered reinforced concrete reservoir with a capacity of 4,500,000 gallons, a new distribution system of cast-iron pipe, two pumping stations and an elevated steel tank with a capacity of 200,000 gallons.

In addition to sources of supply already used, they are adding to the provisions for a potable water supply an important campaign for the drilling of deep wells. There are many Venezuelan experts in well drilling, some of them trained in the petroleum fields. In Maracaibo, under the direction of the water department, they have already put down sixteen deep wells which are producing a volume of 30,000,000 liters per day.

Along with the new water plant in Maracaibo a new sewage system is being installed.

The Department of Public Works has organized a laboratory for testing all materials. It is under the direction of an American expert. It is not only establishing a scientific basis for the government in fixing technical specifications, but it is improving the materials manufactured in Venezuela.

You get some idea of the active attention being paid to these public works when you look at the number of laborers employed by the state.

At the time of the passing of General Gómez, there were 6,500 workers in all categories of public works. There are now over 40,000 Venezuelans engaged on the public pay roll as workers; so many in fact that one cannot help wondering how long the nation's income will be sufficient to continue their employment—how soon many of them will be returned to productive work.

CHAPTER XVII

## Something New in the Treatment of Leprosy

WHEN YOU BEGIN THE DRIVE from La Guaira to Caracas, a very impressive group of buildings, in a secluded nook of the mountains, somewhat distant from the road, excites your first question.

"That's the leprosy colony," tersely answers the driver.

No review of the health problems of Venezuela would be complete if it did not include some consideration of this terrorizing subject.

Every nation in the occidental world isolates leprosy, seeking rigidly to restrain it by reducing its opportunity to spread its infection. In the streets of Kobe, Japan, fifteen years ago, a friend had guided me around a leper who sat on the sidewalk. I've never forgotten my shivers of horror. I was affected by the ancient literatures through which these unhappy ones have been crying out to us for two thousand years, "Unclean, unclean!"

In Venezuela there is something new upon the subject. This land possesses one of the world's few authorities upon the dreadful cutaneous disease.

The discussion by Dr Martin Vegas, of Venezuela, at the International Congress of Leprosy in Cairo in 1938 arrested world-wide attention in the lands where leprosy challenges public safety.

Dr Vegas devoted himself both to the problem of prevention and treatment. As director of the lazar house, he organized the scientific treatment of the disease.

As head of dermatology in the Department of Sanitation and Social Welfare under the government of Venezuela, he has had authority over methods. For years he has been experimenting with chaulmugra oil, reducing its dangerous strength to a point where he has been able to make the taking of it in large doses possible. In Venezuela he has made it compulsory with beneficial effects.

Dr Vegas gave me the following remarkable survey of the subject of leprosy in Venezuela:

"Venezuela has given aid to lepers since the eighteenth century, establishing asylums in the central and eastern regions of the Republic. This is evidenced by the asylums in Caracas, Barcelona and Cumaná.

"At that time it was believed that the purpose of reclusion was to give aid to the leper. It was not done as a prophylactic measure.

"The practice of isolating lepers was maintained throughout the nineteenth century, and three new asylums were established in the west, in the regions where leprosy prevailed.

"At the beginning of the present century this system of small regional lazar houses was 'erroneously' substituted by a system of lazar houses with greater capacity for the concentration of all known patients. Thus the present lazar houses were founded: Cabo Blanco, in the central part of the country near the port of La Guaira, and Providencia, on the island of the same name in Lake Maracaibo. The only apparent reason for the selection of these sites was the facilities for the transportation of the patients by water. On the other hand, sufficient consideration was not given to the various reasons which make the sites chosen undesirable.

"In the last eighteen years these two lazar houses have undergone an important change. Let us see what this change has been: from 1908 to 1920 the patients passed the remaining years of their lives in contemplation of the progress of their disease because medical attention was in its first stage and we might say that it was limited to combatting intercurrent diseases.

"In 1921 treatments were begun on the basis of esters of chaulmugra oils, prepared by one of the chemists in the laboratory of the Department of Public Health, who was sent abroad to study this preparation. There followed a period when the government and the lepers were given high hopes, notwithstanding that very little was known at the time regarding this disease, through a treatment too recent to permit the judging of results in a disease of such dilatory evolution. The excessive enthusiasm of this beginning did not last very long, and a great effort was required to attain the proper concept and a useful orientation.

"In the last few years an endeavor has been made to change the old asylums into the present institutions, which define more clearly their analogy with hospitals because of the intensification of medical activities.

"The buildings were enlarged and modified in order to make them more comfortable and suitable for their new functions. The old pavilions which formerly housed the patients were divided into apartments for two or three patients only. The pavilions for infirmary, laboratory, X-rays and surgery were built, as well as clinics for examination of the patients, files of medical papers, laboratories for ophthalmology, laryngology and dentistry; a plant for purification of sewage waters; housing in the vicinity for the personnel, etc.

"Since our observations coincided with those made in many places where attention has been given to the treatment of leprosy, as regards the importance of general good health in order that the chaulmugra treatment be effective, a plan of organization has been developed, as efficiently as possible, in order that each patient be constantly watched and so that all intercurrent diseases be treated by a select group of physicians.

"Official control for the entry and departure of lepers from the hospitals has been submitted to strict regulation, and we might say that our methods of control are superior to those employed in the lazar houses of Asia and North and South America. We consider this very important, for it is believed that conclusions can be entirely different if the principles that govern such control are different. For example, I was convinced that the deficiency in the examinations made to release Philippine patients is responsible for the high percentage of recurrence. This should not be called recurrence, for patients who were still active had been released.

"The treatment followed in Cabo Blanco from 1926 to 1937 was the subject of detailed study, which I submitted to the International Congress on Leprosy that met in Cairo in March 1938. Our experience led us to the conclusion that there is no reason for giving preference to esters over purified chaulmugra oil. This was tried on over one thousand patients under an entirely regular treatment. The percentages of healing and improvement are higher than, or at least as high as, those of the best-known lazar houses.

"At the present time Venezuela is following a program in its fight against leprosy which has the double objective of improving the condition of the patient in reclusion on the one hand, and, on the other, to control leprosy in the country by means of the recent achievements in epidemiology and prevention of disease."

# CHAPTER XVIII

## Cattle and Their Pests

---

IN A LAND where there is a shortage of human food, the development of the livestock industry seems to offer a direct relief easily accomplished. The improvement of beef animals has in the past received considerable attention in Venezuela.

The Venezuelan cattlemen, a quarter of a century ago, introduced into their herds zebu blood. The zebu is the sacred cow of India, termed Brahman in the United States. By crossing this blood with the creole (*criollo* in Spanish) or native stock, they have developed a very hardy type of beef cattle of fair size, capable of resisting to a great degree the tropical handicaps.

Beef steers at four to five years of age, when most of them are marketed, develop to an average weight of a thousand pounds. Occasionally thirteen hundred pounds is reached, but this weight is the exception. These cattle are somewhat better, on the average, than the so-called Southern native stock of Spanish origin in the United States, such as those found in Florida and other sections of the Gulf country.

A valuable survey in animal husbandry was being made, while I was in Venezuela, by Mr W. H. Black, of the Bureau of Animal Industry, United States Department of Agriculture. An outstanding expert, Mr Black had been invited to make this study at the expense of the Standard Oil Company of Venezuela. The company undertook this project as a useful offering to the Venezuelan livestock interests. Among other things Mr Black was to select areas where the Standard Oil Company was to send some Santa Gertrudis cattle from the King Ranch in Texas in the hope that the beef-producing qualities of the industry in Venezuela would be improved. In addition to the foregoing the company has given helpful attention to the agricultural needs of Venezuela by establishing an agricultural training school at Caripito.

I was with Mr Black in some of his investigations and noted the deep interest of Venezuelan cattlemen in his suggestions.

Mr Black, with high officials of the Ministry of Agriculture and Animal Husbandry, inspected the unloading of a shipment from the United States of thirty-seven white-faced bulls, six heifers and about fifty sheep at Puerto Cabello. They were to be taken to the near-by agricultural stations and given, under careful supervision, a sort of training in the immunities needed for their new environment. Then they were to be used with native stock for the development of cattle of higher beef conformation and quality, and accordingly better food values.

Mr Black, who has studied animal husbandry in various parts of the world, realized that you couldn't breed successfully against the pests of this tropical country a purebred beef animal of the highly bred British breeds until something had been done to reduce the dangers and tests under which the animal must live, any more than you could raise, without special precautions, a purebred animal in some of the semitropical sections of the Southern states.

He explained that the severest pest in Venezuela is the larva which comes from a species of fly called *Dermatobia hominis,* commonly known as "nuche" or "torsalo." This pest extends all the way from northern Argentina to Central America. Fortunately it has not appeared in the United States.

The pest causes lumps, which are larvae, under the hide of the animal, similar in appearance to the condition caused by ox warbles in the United States. Our ox warbles are confined to the backs of the cattle. The ox warble fly lays its eggs on the animal's legs, where they hatch and penetrate the hide. They then migrate through the muscles and finally appear on the backs of the cattle. Therefore, when you see these lumps on the backs of the United States stock, you realize that they injure the hide and reduce the vitality of the animal. However, they cause less damage than the "torsalo" or "nuche" of South and Central America, because the damaged area is confined to the backs of the cattle, whereas the "nuche" affects all areas of the animal.

The "torsalo," which is bigger than the house fly, lays eggs upon the bellies of mosquitoes. Don't ask me how. The government entomologist has caught them at it, and this is his statement. The mosquitoes attack the cow, and the larvae are formed in the egg while still on the body of the mosquito. This larva may remain in the eggshell for fifteen days before protruding. The egg is provided with a little valvelike opening, or window. When the cow's hair extends to the valve opening of the egg, the larvae descend down the hair, reach the cow's hide and penetrate it through the puncture made by the mosquito. They then develop rapidly, causing large swellings and becoming full-sized grubs three quarters of an inch in length. They cover the animal almost completely in extreme cases.

When the larva reaches full development, it leaves the animal and falls to the ground and in due time becomes a fly ready to prey on some convenient cow.

Meanwhile it has left the animal weakened, made a sieve out of the cow's hide and ruined much of the carcass.

The pest is more prevalent in the humid area along the streams than in the open savannahs.

When Mr Black was asked the remedy, he said, "The parasite will persist as long as mosquitoes act as carriers. The big job is to eradicate either the fly or the mosquito, which acts as carrier for torsalo. It is another Gorgas job."

It is not uncommon for the human to become infested with this worm. You see many victims of it in the llanos country. A simple yet effective remedy is to put a piece of fat pork on the lump; the larva comes out in about two hours.

The first step to cattle improvement is in better care of the stock. Little attention has been given to either breeding or management. Few dipping vats have been installed. Mr Black reminded me that a quarter of a century ago or less we had trouble introducing dipping vats in many of the sections infested with cattle ticks in our Southern states.

The government now is giving considerable attention to the subject of animal husbandry and to further its program has brought experts in livestock and plant breeding from various parts of the world, hoping to make speed in the development of this vital industry in a land which now imports much of its food, including meat. These experts are introducing several breeds of beef cattle. About six rather large importations have been made since August 1938. They are also importing good specimens of many dairy breeds. These foreign cattle are usually brought to the Maracay station to be immunized, after which they are distributed to the various government livestock stations over the nation. Nine of these stations have been created during recent years, and the government is planning to develop some added centers of livestock study and development.

The first experiment of the government calls for the co-operation of the individual cattlemen. The government will furnish the service of the bulls to the Venezuelan owners, who bring their cows to the experiment station for free service. The first effort of the crossbreeding will be to improve the native or creole cattle.

Said Mr Black, "Too much cannot be said about the staying qualities of the creole cow. She has successfully fought every Venezuelan pest. For years she will undoubtedly remain the foundation of the cattle stock of Venezuela."

While the improvement of crossbreeding will be slow, it will be continuous and progressive.

When I asked Mr Black what made the Venezuelan meat so tough, he gave me to understand that it was not the fault of the creole cow entirely, but that it was partially due to the butcher, who seldom is experienced in cutting meat as the North Americans desire it.

"Meat," said he, "is slaughtered in a primitive way, outside of the government abattoirs, where only a small percentage of it is handled."

The Venezuelan butcher apparently does not realize that cutting the meat against or across the grain has a direct relationship to its tenderness. He hacks it in any way, cutting most of it with the grain, which may make the most tender meat in the world tough, unless perhaps much attention is given to the cooking of it.

Another thing which, in Mr Black's opinion, militates against good results in meat production is that through generations here Venezuelans have wanted their meat fresh from the kill. The native population, as a rule, knows very little about frozen meat.

As Mr Black talked to me about this, I remembered that I had ridden in a passenger automobile a few days before from Maracay to Caracas. We went through villages and small towns, passing frequent places where fresh meat was hung up in the open for sale. One of my fellow passengers kept stopping the car, getting out and buying these fresh products of primitive slaughter. By the time we reached Caracas he had legs of lamb and loins of beef scattered all over his immediate vicinity in the car.

The Washington expert in animal husbandry thought that something could be done in Venezuela for the improvement of livestock feed to meet the persistent invasion of the pastures by wire grass. All the livestock stations are doing a lot of work with improved grasses.

The cattlemen are taking a more intelligent interest in the handling of the stock. The more progressive ranchers castrate their bull calves, to which function they were once indifferent. They are under the spell of the experts, who fortunately have caught their attention.

In discussing this matter, Mr Black makes, in his report, this observation:

"Greater attention should be given to the numbers and types of bulls used in beef production. On most of the large ranches hundreds of inferior bulls, many showing dairy breeding, are in use. One rancher reported having 14,000 cows, and when asked how many bulls he was using with these cows, replied, 'There are just as many bulls as cows.' There is a tendency to use dairy bulls, particularly Holsteins, in many range herds kept principally for beef production. This condition exists because nearly every rancher makes some cheese. It would be much more desirable to select the best milking cows and keep them as dairy cows, breeding them to a bull of dairy breeding, rather than to use dairy bulls promiscuously in the range beef herd.

"The results in the use of improved beef-bred bulls by the animal-husbandry experiment stations should be fruitful in the course of a few years through the demonstration of the value of crossbred types for different locations."

There seems to be no very good reason why, in time, with the enlargement of the livestock areas, the cattle raisers of Venezuela should not provide the major meat supply which now is provided by foreign countries.

Mr Black also points out in his report some encouraging developments in improved dairies near the larger cities. There are approximately 165 dairies near Caracas alone, in which over five thousand cows are milked. Most of the milk sold in Caracas is pasteurized.

Most of the dairies have imported a considerable

number of Holstein, Jersey and Guernsey cattle. The first-mentioned breed seems to be the most popular.

The native cow still predominates in the dairy herds. While not a large producer, she averages at best about seven pounds daily for the lactation period, and her milk contains about 4 per cent of fat. Fat, however, is of little concern at the present time, as cream is not generally used on the table; cheese is more popular than butter in the diet.

The ranchers with whom Mr Black stayed during his investigation showed him several new tricks. One was the custom of tying the calf to the dam's left front leg during the time the cow is actually milked, in order that the presence of the calf may inspire the mother to give her milk more freely. Another had to do with Mr Black's morning coffee. The farmer would bring out a large mug with hot concentrated coffee in it and would sit down on the milking stool and fill the mug full of foaming milk fresh from the cow's udder. Mr Black said it looked like a glorified ice-cream soda—but he didn't tell me how it tasted!

The gradual improvement which Mr Black noticed in cattle and dairying extends somewhat to other features of agriculture.

Coffee is the leading crop. Its exports have a value of over $10,000,000 a year, the United States being the largest customer. The United States also absorbs a high percentage of the cacao, bananas, and practically all the pig and goat skins. But it will be a long time before there is, in Venezuela, an exportable surplus of meat and agricultural commodities. Outside of petroleum, which constitutes 80 per cent of its total exports, Venezuela is an importing country.

# CHAPTER XIX

## *The Remarkable Emphasis on Education*

---

THE RECENTLY COMPLETED Ministry of Education
building, a six-story edifice, towers above the two-story
city of Caracas like a skyscraper. At the moment, it is
the handsomest of the homes of the various ministries.
Nearly every minister told me about the new building
which is expected to be constructed for his department
as soon as they get to it.

The Ministry of Education building is built out of
native material where granite and stone abound; where
mahogany and ebony are as common as soft pine in the
United States. Its tiled floors reflect the gift of the
Latin peoples in making beautiful mosaics.

The entrance of the building contains an elaborate
marble rotunda in which have been placed the busts
of scholars famous in letters and education in Venezuelan history.

The building has an air of such finished beauty that
at first glance it looks more like a place for exhibition

than for work. But on every floor I found well-appointed offices, full of young men and women who scarcely took their eyes off what they were doing.

Everybody seemed in a hurry. There was no tropical tempo in this Ministry of Education.

Dr Enrique Tejera, the minister, is a man of wide culture, who came home from Paris, where he was pursuing medical research, to take this place in the cabinet.

"When the present program was launched," said he, "we had to rent buildings to supplement our needs. Our first order for equipment was for fifty-two thousand school desks from the United States. We have since placed an order for an additional eighty thousand American school desks. As rapidly as we master the technique of it, we will make some desks of our own."

I looked out of the window and could see mahogany trees. I observed that the American desks were made of steel painted to represent mahogany. There ought to be no reason why the native school desks to be created in the future will not mark an advance in the beauty of furniture.

The minister explained to me: "In 1935 there were two thousand schools in primary education in Venezuela; now there are over four thousand schools. There were then nineteen hundred school teachers; now there are over six thousand."

There were in 1935 about one hundred thousand pupils registered; now more than four hundred thousand must be provided with primary education, and they have merely begun to touch the population of school age.

The minister, in discussing this fact, said, "We are not meeting our growing need, but we are showing progress. We shall increase the schools as we increase our corps of teachers. As rapidly as they are trained, we are providing new schools."

The pupils in secondary education under schools controlled by the ministry have been multiplying by over 300 per cent.

Dr Alej. Alfonzo-Larrain, the director of Pedagogical Extension, who had studied in Columbia University, gave me an interesting discussion of the extension department just established in Venezuelan education. It has three branches—educational radio, educational motion pictures, and correspondence courses. On a wall in his office was a large map of Venezuela. It was pockmarked with tacks of various colors which indicate the stages through which these three systems of education are developing.

The correspondence courses have proceeded as far west as the foothills of the Andean mountains and to the very border of Colombia. In some places he would have only one student taking a correspondence course. In Maracaibo he had something over twenty. Altogether, several hundred new students were being introduced to this new program of correspondence courses each month. These courses were ordered as an effort to intensify the broadening of primary education. They were expected to be of assistance to teachers in distant locations in the country where there is no possible opportunity to follow a normal course. The courses, which started to function only in 1939, use subjects corresponding to the first year of primary normal instruction.

The educational radio reaches the most distant points of the national territory, appealing both to aspirant teachers and to school children. Special courses in teaching and in general knowledge, which otherwise it would be impossible for them to acquire through any other medium in their far-off places, are given at regular hours. The educational radio broadcasts daily in hours that correlate with the class schedule of the schools.

The broadcasting program comprises such subjects as geology, Spanish, history, hygiene, gymnasium, civics, natural sciences and elementary arts. A special weekly program has also been arranged for broadcasting which depicts the life of the most notable men of the world, with emphasis upon those of Venezuela.

A practical phase of the educational radio also instructs its pupils how to administer first aid in cases of emergency, instruction that is exceedingly useful in remote parts of the country where there are few doctors.

Lectures, comedies, and various entertainments are broadcast regularly. The lectures are intended specifically to help the children's relatives, who are also pupils of the extension courses, in guiding their education after school hours.

There is a question box where all queries asked by teachers in regard to their profession are answered. A course in pedagogy is also given to them through this medium, with practical demonstrations of the new theories in education. In order to contribute more fully to the efficiency of the educational radio, the Minister of National Education has supplied hundreds of schoolhouses in the country with radios.

Three kinds of institutions define clearly the meanings and bearings of Rural Education in Venezuela. They are: the rural normal school "El Macaro," the rural school "Tamanaco," and the "Central Rural Mission."

The rural normal school "El Macaro" has been founded with the sole purpose of habilitating and capacitating rural teachers for schools of this kind already functioning in Venezuela and for those that are to be created in the future. The importance of this institution is plainly seen when it is known that, up to this day, Venezuela never had a single rural teacher that could be said to be technically prepared for this class of instruction. In order to assure the students a thorough capacitation at the rural normal school "El Macaro," the Ministry of National Education has disposed that the duration of the courses taught shall be three years. The first year comprises the subjects of the sixth grade of primary education. The second year is a course of rural technique, with which it is intended to equip the rural teachers in such way that they will create in the peasants' consciences the necessity and convenience of being actively incorporated in the social and economic life of the nation. The third year is a course integrated exclusively with pedagogic matters and could be called a professional course.

To fulfill properly the ends for which it was established, the rural normal school "El Macaro" is not only a perfect example when considered in its technical organization, but also—and this is more important—in its material aspect.

The ministry has classified into two categories the rural schools it intends to establish in various parts of the country. They are called "complete" and "incomplete." The first of the "complete" to be established is the rural school "Tamanaco." The first of the "incomplete" is in Prin, Colonia Bejarano, and is known as "Sorocaima." In one and the other the Ministry of National Education is making experiments that embrace all the aspects of its organization with the purpose of accomplishing, within a certain time, the definite structure of the rural schools of Venezuela.

The pupils attending these schools are the children of peasants and rural workers and therefore the most recipient of the kind of instruction taught at these schools. It is superfluous to say, besides the subjects related with handcraft arts, the rural schools furnish instruction also in agriculture, cattle raising, trades, rural industrialization, dressmaking and sewing. To facilitate and make practical the teaching of these subjects, the rural schools are furnished with pigsties, hencoops, warrens, pigeon houses, beehives and a vast experimental field.

The Minister of National Education does not neglect the need of continuing the preparation and proper capacitation of the teachers of the rural schools now in service. To this effect he has ordered the creation of the "Central Rural Mission" under the direct control of an Assistant Commissioner of Rural Education, one of whose duties it is to organize and direct the functioning of a number of rural schools already grouped in what is called the First Rural Circuit.

The orientation given to the "Central Rural Mission" determines in part the scope of the tasks to be undertaken by the rural school missioners, now at the rural school "El Macaro," where they were appointed to study a capacitation course before starting to work as rural teachers.

I went from the Ministry of Education to the "Instituto de Pedagógico"—teachers' college. It was an artistic new building capable of accommodating several hundred students. One wing was for the education of professors of high schools, another was for professors and teachers of grade schools. Other rooms were set apart for the special instruction of teachers in advanced courses in mathematics, languages and physics, and with emphasis upon the ever-present importance of geology. It was really three schools in one, because, in addition to the training of high-school professors and common-school teachers, there were classes in regular high-school work, and the building, which had been opened only a month, was humming with activity.

Every student is required to have two years of chemistry, two years of physics, two years of philosophy and two years of biology.

The equipment was thoroughly modern and complete. There was a Steinway piano in the chapel; and on the desks, wardrobes, lockers and other equipment in schoolrooms, laboratories, rest rooms and even the gymnasium, I saw the ever-comforting sign of the Grand Rapids manufacturer.

There were large chemical laboratories, and there was a very complete installation of equipment for the teaching of domestic science in a room especially designed. In every school I visited in any part of Venezuela, even in the rural districts, I found this emphasis upon domestic science.

I observed that the building was air conditioned. Caracas is three thousand feet above the sea level, and its climate is comfortable at all times of the day and night. There are only two seasons in Venezuela—the wet season and the dry season. Unless you are on the seashore or in the coastal valleys, the heat is not intense at any time. So I asked the director of the school why the government had gone to the great expense of installing air conditioning in a climate so comfortable. It was the most up to date and elaborate system made in the United States and must have cost a lot of money.

The reply of the director surprised me. Said he, "We do not use air conditioning in these school buildings as a matter of comfort, but as a prophylactic. Every new school building will be air conditioned. The land is full of communicable diseases, and according to scientific opinion the constant changing of the air in the schoolrooms will do much to prevent the spread of germs."

Connected with the new Pedagogical Institute was a wide athletic field, larger than a city block, with the beginnings of what apparently will be an ornate stadium. Already championship material in baseball, football and basketball is being developed. Every Venezuelan boy knows the name of Chauvez, who has challenged the champion boxer of the United States for the championship.

Too much cannot be said of the care the Ministry of Education has taken to emphasize the outdoor features of the program in the country, where everybody stays out of doors as much of the time as possible. Right across from the new schoolhouse what was once a commercial recreation dance pavilion has been torn down, and in its place tennis courts have been constructed.

In a streamlined new three-story building next to the Pedagogical Institute I went to visit the latest word in Venezuela's broadcasting stations, of which there are several, all prosperous under individual ownership. This station was owned in part by a member of the Chamber of Deputies. He was not having any trouble with censorship, and thought the radio freedom in Venezuela broader than that in the United States. In a land where only 7½ per cent of the population read the newspapers, there is a natural territory for the radio. During the past three and a half years this feature of transmission has been one of the most rapidly growing private endeavors in the nation.

I have never seen so many types of education under one roof as I discovered when I entered a palatial new building which had chiseled on its front, in modern art letters, "Venezuela." I had been passing it for several days, realizing dimly that it was a schoolhouse and that eventually I should travel through its mammoth spaces.

It has a thousand pupils. Its courses cover the entire school survey from kindergarten, beginning at four years of age, up through the grades, stopping by the way to experiment in practically every avenue of human knowledge which relates to prevocational courses.

I visited one of the higher grade classes where the students were discussing the new revolution in Bolivia, which had that day gone from a so-called republic to a dictatorship. They were discussing it with restraint, confining themselves rather largely to the spot news and historical features of the story.

They did not discuss the "isms." But one pupil read a patriotic essay upon the benefits of the Pan American Union.

Suddenly I heard a strain of radio music broadcast from some central point in the building. Immediately the pupils arose, indicating that the music was the recess bell.

I discovered later that this building of many rooms is controlled from this broadcast station. No bells ever ring. Strains of music denote the recess periods, the periods at which classes change, and the retirement from the building at the close of the day. The radio control is the building control. The school has a special system of loudspeakers in every classroom, and the transmission can be controlled from the office of the principal. There are two concerts transmitted weekly through this medium to all classes.

Another manifestation I had never witnessed before was the attitude of the pupils toward recess. On this occasion they continued discussing Bolivia. Probably not 10 per cent of them left the room, and when in fifteen minutes some strains of music came from the broadcast room, it didn't require much shifting for the classes for studies to proceed. The director explained to me that I was witnessing an indication of the interest which the students have in their work.

I was taken to a room where pupils in the art of sculpture were making plastic figures; to a room where a Russian girl and a well-known pianist were teaching the pupils rhythm through a process of dancing and singing.

Significant of the government's concern over the subject of diet was a tiled, well-aired room for the teaching of domestic science, with its modern equipment. Here free lunches and pure milk are served to the poorer underfed children.

I was told that in establishing this school, the authorities had taken some of their ideas from the Lincoln School of New York. They have completed in this experimental school a system of education in which rotate three separate and distinct kinds of instruction: manual, academic and laboratory.

We visited one room where the pupils, with curiously expectant faces, were looking at a cabinet in a corner. As we entered, the teacher stepped to the door of the cabinet, opened it, and a little brown pupil came out.

"Is it for punishment?" I asked.

"No," replied the director. "We are studying the air, and this little experiment was to indicate how long the child might remain, without ill effects, in that closed cabinet consuming the oxygen. The purpose is to impress the pupils with the importance of ample air space in which to live."

There was a printing plant where these Venezuelan pupils get out a daily newspaper in colors, making from linoleum the color blocks, setting up the type, and doing the presswork.

I encountered one phase of classification which possesses a peculiar proof of how thoroughly modernized the educational system has become—some testing rooms where experts were grading the responsiveness of the pupils. It was altogether a process to determine the speed and facility with which the pupils digest their courses, and seemed to me to be fully as expert as the plan for classification of students under which the Progressive Education Association is sponsoring such a testing program in thirty schools in the United States. These tests were carried on, not by studying the previous grades—many of these pupils had no previous grades—but by continuously employing the utmost patience and time necessary to secure the most useful classification, so that the slow pupils will not hold back the swifter ones.

That Venezuela is doing for all its schools what selected groups in this country are doing with special schools, indicates that it is highly progressive and coming well to the front educationally. While its system is much younger than most others, it is in line with the best schools of all countries.

This experimental school is being duplicated in other centers of population of the nation. It expresses the plan of Venezuela to develop an educational program that will meet the peculiar conditions prevailing in this country. Primary education constitutes the biggest problem, owing to the thousands of illiterate children.

These "Activity Schools," as they are called by the educators of Venezuela, are able to ignore the relative ages and conglomerate experiences of the children.

Said the Minister of Education in discussing the experimental school:

"Its principal aim is to build an individual and collective conscience of economic, social, esthetic and ethical values. To attain this end it employs, as an important medium, the experiences of the students, and they acquire their knowledge through observation and in the laboratories.

"In other aspects of their social life, the students act always independently and for themselves; they make their laws; they have their courts of justice; they form in groups and organize corporations; they write their own newspapers and form social clubs.

"The school presents to the students a field of cultural values duly organized which allow them to take advantage of the opportunity to develop their vocations, at the same time not abandoning other activities which they are compelled to utilize outside their natural inclinations.

"The cultural environment of the students constitutes the main purpose of the school, and to this end the Activity School responds in this way:

"By estimating the vocational possibilities of the students in order that each shall follow the cultural activities suitable to his liking and temperament—as this is the most sensible manner in which the child will get a proper education in the school.

"The methodological base is constituted by the coordination of developing processes and learnings about 'Centros de Interés,' in accordance with the theories of Decroly, Dewey, Kirchenteiner, Radice and others—

though adapted to the mentality and character of our children.

"Such adaptation consists in the suppression of the grades and in the increase of teachers attending to their various vocational activities. As a substitute for the 'only environment,' there is the laboratory for the sciences, the lecture hall, the workshops, for the literary, social and economic pursuits. A highly trained staff of teachers is in charge of music, plastics, rhythmics and the juvenile theater."

As we came away from this astounding school a clever member of the Chamber of Deputies, who had accompanied the party, said, "This nation has literally jumped from diapers to long pants."

The day I left Venezuela, the municipal council of the Federal District of Caracas placed its final approval upon the construction of a recreation center for youth at Catia La Mar, a beautiful beach not far from La Guaira. This is to provide a year-around opportunity for three hundred boys and three hundred girls to spend two weeks each on the beach. Their eligibility to enjoy these privileges is fixed by the municipal schools they attend within the Federal District. Every pupil from five years of age to fifteen who attends any grade in the municipal school is entitled to the advantages of the sea colony.

I was shown the plans which embrace two very large buildings of this recreation center, each structure having a 264-foot front and extending back in wings 160

feet long and two stories in height. The structures will
be fireproof. These "School Colonies on the Sea," as
they are known, will cost something like 500,000 bolivars. The disbursement will be liquidated out of taxes
which are called municipal rents. There are no ad-
valorem property taxes in Venezuela, but all real estate
in the Federal District pays a small rental tax. It is
estimated that these taxes, collected as the school colonies are being constructed, will meet the outlay by the
time the buildings are ready for occupancy.

Provisions for nurses and athletic coaches are made.
Each teacher will accompany her own pupils on recreation.

It is estimated that by using the six hundred accommodations available the year around, this municipal
recreation center will touch over thirty thousand school
children a year.

The social justification of the institution arises out of
the fact that 65 per cent of the people of Venezuela
belong to the poorer working class and have not been
able to give their children the attention desirable. This
holiday of two weeks for every school child in the
Federal District is provided by the district government, and includes medical attention, a scientifically
balanced diet, and a period during which every child is
placed under the observation of trained physicians and
nurses.

The governor of Caracas, whose love for children is
well known, has thought out the details. Among the

minor considerations, he has insisted that regulation uniforms shall be provided to the children by the state in order that the poorer children, whose shabby clothes might make them sensitive, shall have no cause to worry about their appearance when they go to the colony.

# CHAPTER XX

## *Art Schools and Artists*

---

IT WAS NATURAL that the cultural imagination should have been stirred by the educational developments of the new republican government. There has been a general release of artistic and intellectual activities in Venezuela during recent years.

Many young people are writing, and the Venezuelan publications are brilliant with examples of wit and satire directed against age-old evils. The modern Venezuelan writer seems to be a man of little faith in the pretenses of the new day and with no taste for the accomplishments of the old days.

Venezuela has officially recognized the ability of young artists, painters, composers and writers by giving them administrative positions. For example, Luis Lopez Mendez holds an important position in the Bureau of Culture and Fine Arts.

There is one great name in fiction, Romulo Gallegos, whose novel, *Doña Barbara,* was a genuine contribution to literature. It gave to the Orinoco ranch life as distinctive a flavor as some of the United States writers have given to Western literature.

Amongst the vehicles of expression that have been created under the spirit of the new freedom are some remarkable samples of modernistic woodcarving that have taken their places in the galleries.

The sculptor Francisco Narvaez is one of the strongest influences in Venezuela's contemporaneous artistic movement. The National Museum of Fine Arts of Venezuela recently has acquired one of his splendid works. To the credit of Narvaez is the beautiful fountain in the park at Carabobo. Some of his architectural modeling is also used on the outer walls of the Fine Arts Museum in Caracas.

Venezuela also produced, a generation ago, one of the best women pianists the world has ever known, Maria Teresa Carreno.

One of the places growing famous in the educational system is the art school. They refer to it as the "Plastic Arts." When you have gone through it, you realize that there isn't any department of art which it does not cover. When I went into the entrance hall of the institution, the first thing that struck me was a notice to members of the alumni that a contest was on among the students of painting for sixteen scholarships. The successful contestants were to be privileged to study painting in schools in Chile and Mexico. They would receive their transportation and one hundred bolivars a month for their expenses while studying.

The institution emphasizes ceramics, seeking to improve the output of the ancient potteries, investigating Indian resources, and standardizing a practical knowledge which will be of use to a pottery industry. The boys are being taught how to make their own ovens, develop their own colors and burn their own vessels.

Though this art school was not begun until July 1938, it now has a large attendance. Recently the enrollment of the school has increased something like one hundred per month.

There is an interesting department of textiles, with a night course in interior decorating. A large class is being taught modeling; there are several classes in painting.

Miss Claire, an American girl, is in charge of a department engaged in weaving yarns, completing Indian rugs, and developing the work to a point where it will be useful as an industry. An Indian teacher was occupied in showing the students how to make floor matting out of coarse fiber and loose weaving. Out of sheep's wool in natural colors they were making remarkable black-and-white rugs.

It was the most variegated art school I had ever seen. In one room the making of fabrics, in another the modeling of figures, in another a large class in painting with native models, in another the teaching of graphic arts, in another special work in leather, and in another the making of blocks, tiles, mosaics and art glass.

The pupils were all enthusiastic: I was told that out of the miscellaneous effort of the whole there was growing an atmosphere that will result in the building of a new structure of sufficient capacity to house and develop the variety of talent now making its way in the somewhat heterogeneous atmosphere of the institution referred to under the inadequate title of "Plastic Arts."

☆      ☆      ☆

Two graceful institutions stand opposite each other on the beautiful road through the mahogany forest between Caracas and the country club. They are of recent construction. One is called the "Museum of Arts," the other the "Museum of Sciences."

The Museum of Sciences had just been finished and the furniture was being moved in when I visited the place. The Museum of Arts was completed, and into it had been moved many art treasures. It is a young gallery, but its setting is a rarely beautiful one, and its art collections embrace some fine paintings.

There is an interesting organization of artists in Venezuela called "A Circle of Fine Arts." Those in the group include such well-known figures in the art world as Romulo Gallegas, Julio and Enrique Planchart, Maldonado, Martinez, Castillo, Brandt, Caravano, Reveron and Manuel Cabre.

The artist Armando Reveron is an educated man from a family of class and standing in Caracas. After studying art in the regular schools at home and in Paris, he lived abroad many years. Coming back to his birthplace, he reverted to nature.

He lives in a native thatched hut, or rather in a group of them, on the coast at Macuto. He built them himself —of sticks, stones, burlap and palm thatches. He bound them together with mud in the primitive way, since he possesses an obsession against hammer and nails and other hard surfaces.

Two of these huts are studios crowded with his own paintings and workshop properties, all jumbled together in confusion. An Indian woman, who was a servant in his mother's household, poses as a model for many of his paintings and superintends his simple daily needs.

The artist wears scanty clothing the year around. The day I visited him, his bare feet were encased in a pair of homemade sandals; his shirt was absent; his only other garment was a pair of burlap trunks. In the tropical climate of the Caribbean seacoast, it was ample. He was burned a dark brown, looked healthy, and his fine eyes and chiseled features, which gave him the look of an aesthete, redeemed his personality from the obvious misrepresentation of his crude surroundings.

I had been told that he was reluctant to show his paintings. Therefore his simple and unconscious willingness in exhibiting a great number of them seemed to be a special courtesy of the occasion.

There were dozens of them, scattered through the

*Central University of Venezuela, Caracas.*

two good-sized huts—some were behind doors or hidden under the rude furniture, others were covered by oddly fashioned lay figures or hiding behind improvised easels. How he ever disposed of them in such utter confusion, I did not have time to observe. He delved nimbly from one pile of litter to another, and always came up with a picture.

Reveron's palette consists of various tones of white, his paintbrushes are mostly stumps from which the bristles are gone; sometimes he stops to replenish the almost bare surface of his paintbrush with something to which the paint will cling, then he works on.

The surroundings of his work place and the eccentricities of his person do not prepare you for the astonishing result he produces upon the canvas. An educated artist who has studied widely, his works are known in galleries in Europe, particularly in Paris, where they appear in national exhibits. His paintings express a strong originality of spirit. The delicacy of his work, revealed in the whites and grays of his palette, presents the influence of his study of the Impressionists, although there is little trace of the Impressionists in his actual work. There is an originality all his own in his productions, expressed in his personal co-ordination of artistic elements. His use of lights reaches an ascendancy of white shades which suggests a similarity to Carrière.

He sells great numbers of his paintings for good prices—and his neighbors gossip as to what he does with the money. It is said that the government paid him a good many thousand bolivars for the paintings he made especially for the Venezuelan exhibit at the 1939 World's Fair in New York.

Venezuelan society continues interested in this man who holds aloof from it. They never knew what changed his viewpoint in life and sent him into the peculiar solitude in which he carries on a conspicuous work. My companion, René Borges, whose introductions were responsible for the visit with Reveron, had known him as a boyhood friend and was one of the few men for whom Reveron retains a warm friendship. But even Borges did not know why this rare genius has taken refuge in the primitive life.

Another interesting character in the art world is Mendez, one of the youngest of Venezuelan artists. He spent several years away from home, studying and gathering experience in the Old World. It is his aim to have art in all its various phases reach the masses in his native country.

This young artist uses strong contrasts in color to obtain the local flavor of his land. It is believed his influence is destined to have a far-reaching effect in spreading art throughout Venezuela.

Any account of the artistic geniuses of the modern day should mention Tito Salus, an outstanding exemplar of the nineteenth-century tradition.

In discussing the cultural life of Venezuela, you are reminded that there are several institutions of higher learning, some of which have age-old traditions. The University of Caracas was organized before Harvard. The University of Mérida was an ancient school of Spanish culture before Bolívar arrived. These universities have splendid reputations in which higher education has used its opportunities, unfortunately, for the education of classes rather than masses. They have held to the old-time Spanish purpose that higher education should be limited to the development of gentlemen scholars. The growing spirit of democracy, as well as the increasing desire for an educational utility, is producing a modern tendency toward the more liberal spread of higher culture.

# CHAPTER XXI

## *Transportation Barriers and Plans to Conquer Them*

LAND TRANSPORTATION has from the beginning been physically the most difficult objective of Venezuela's program. Upon its ultimate solution depend in a general way the future development of agriculture and industry and, in a more specific way, the food supply and other living necessities of the people.

When the ancient upheavals which produced the Andean ranges struck the land which is now Venezuela, they created not only the incredible reservoirs which placed her third in the world's supply of oil, but built immense ranges and high plateaus.

A wing of the Andes, beginning in the southwest corner of Venezuela, runs northeastward in a slow curve across the central and northern portion of the country until it reaches the Caribbean coast line and frowns down upon the sea at La Guaira.

That you may sense the transportation difficulties,

contemplate the fact that it is only seven miles from the port city of La Guaira to Caracas. After your motorcar has circled the mountainside on a spiral road until it reaches the little valley in which the capital is located, your speedometer indicates that you have traveled twenty-three miles to go forward seven miles as the crow flies, into the interior—to come finally to a valley three thousand feet above the level of the sea, separated from the coast by a range of mountains eight to ten thousand feet high.

The wing of the Andes in which lies this terrain is called the Cordillera de la Costa. The Andean vertebrae had separated partially about midway across Venezuela, letting down into a pass some fifteen hundred feet above the level of the sea. The western and southern vertebra which connects this pass with the main range of the Andes is called the Cordillera de los Andes. Together they have piled the land to heights reaching sixteen thousand feet in southwestern and northern and nine thousand feet in eastern Venezuela, leaving high valleys between lofty peaks.

The altitude of these valleys affords an attractive climate, with a rich soil capable of producing the food crops of both tropical and temperate zones. People unfamiliar with tropical climates do not always realize the importance of the altitudes which give to the so-called Torrid Zone continual surprises relative to climate.

Temperatures in the Torrid Zone are determined by

altitude above the sea, if there are no local variations
due to special topographical influences.

Dr Bunker, the consulting engineer of the water-
supply program in Venezuela, called our attention
to the fact, as an example, that in Ecuador, through
which the equator passes, there are many regions with
characteristics of the temperate zone at elevations varying from seventy-five hundred to ten thousand feet
above the sea level. Quito, the capital of Ecuador,
situated almost on the equator at an altitude of 9,343
feet above the sea level, has an average annual temperature of 55 degrees. In contrast, Guayaquil, the
principal port of Ecuador, while only 288 miles from
Quito, being located near the sea level, has a mean
annual temperature of 81.5 degrees.

Venezuela, though farther away from the equator,
furnishes a similar example of climatic contrast. The
lowlands, including the coastal plains, and the valleys
of the larger rivers are hot. Above the lowlands a cooler
climate is found in valleys and slopes lying at altitudes
of from fifteen hundred to seventy-five hundred feet
above the sea level. Some of the districts in these valleys,
sometimes designated as the subtropical zone, possess a
climate as salubrious as that encountered in the Rocky
Mountain regions at altitudes of from three to five thousand feet. In fact, within a few hours' travel you can get
in Venezuela any temperature you wish, from the torrid
heat of the tropics to the freezing cold of the mountain
tops.

The varied topography of Venezuela therefore provides not only ample scope for general agriculture, but great pasture lands which make possible the development of animal husbandry. Both the livestock and agriculture nevertheless languish because of the distances one must travel over mountain roads.

The mountains everywhere, except in the valley of Lake Maracaibo between the Venezuelan Andes and the Colombian Andes, challenge the highway engineer, and in the Orinoco valley and the llanos large areas subject to flooding make his task difficult.

Gómez, who knew Venezuela like a book and therefore fully understood her transportation needs, wanted a Trans-Andean Highway from Caracas to the Colombian border. He constructed an all-weather road.

It is a practical and very wonderful highway, and the Colombians have extended it from the Venezuelan border on to their capital at Bogotá. It is probably the ruggedest ride in the world, but it met an urgent need to bring San Cristóbal in touch with Caracas. This Trans-Andean Highway, when improved, will be the outstanding feature in the new trans-Andean system. It has unimproved but passable connections from Barquisimeto and Carora to Coro and Maracaibo. A connecting link to Maracaibo from Mototan will be inaugurated in 1940. A trunk-line highway from Valencia by way of San Carlos, Acarigua and Barinas to San Cristóbal was also undertaken by Gómez. Part of this can now be traversed most of the year, but is out of business much of the time in the rainy season. The section from Valencia to Barinas is graveled and passable at all times.

A further trunk line takes off from the Trans-Andean Highway at Cagua near Maracay and passes through San Juan de los Morros, El Sombrero, Valle de la Pascua and Pariaguan to Ciudad Bolívar, thence via Upata, Guasipati, El Callao (where the gold mines are located) and Tumeremo to El Dorado. Eventually this will be extended to the Grand Savannah. From Valle de la Pascua and Pariaguan connecting highways with eastern Venezuela are being improved.

Since the building of the Trans-Andean Highway, Venezuela, and the rest of the world as well, has gone a long way in the intelligent conception of road building.

The office of the Direction of Ways of Communication has, under the leadership of Dr Francisco J. Sucre, a direct descendant of the famous Marshal Sucre, made over 255 technical studies and field surveys. A laboratory for testing materials functions in connection with the bureau. An American expert was engaged for this service, and the laboratory is excellently equipped to test the qualities of materials. This was the first scientific step to improve the materials manufactured or used in the country, and to establish bases for the formulation of better technical specifications for highway and other construction.

The program of highway construction now going forward with reasonable speed also includes extensive

*A road in the Andes.*

construction of paved streets in the larger towns and cities.

A power which overcomes mountains has arrived. Within the last three years, the number of motorized vehicles has increased in Venezuela from fifteen thousand to thirty thousand. Wherever I went, whether in smooth country or rough, in areas populous or unpeopled, I found new automobiles. At Atures, in the remote sparsely populated territory of the Amazonas, I was given a ride in a new Buick car. The Indian driver carried a spade. The road reminded me of the terrains I had jounced over in Iowa, Kansas and Missouri less than a quarter of a century ago.

On our drive, counting the stops to fill up ditches which needed to be made passable, we averaged about fifteen miles an hour. In the old days at home I seldom did any better than this, and the cars of those days were more efficient for bad roads than are the modern low-hung models. They had high wheels and a body sufficiently lifted from the ground to avoid many of the obstacles of an unfinished highway.

Frequently my companions said that as soon as the roads were improved they would get some more cars. It was given to me to bestow upon them the significance of history, namely, that good roads do not bring cars: cars bring good roads. It was so in the United States; it will be so in Venezuela, no matter what mountain heights or flooded valleys are to be crossed by new roads.

✯          ✯          ✯

As long ago as 1930 the Department of Commerce in Washington reported that Venezuela had made much progress in highway construction during the preceding few years and stated that "Venezuela is in the front rank among South American countries in modern highways, taking into consideration population, area and natural resources." With the substantial additions, including those made by the oil companies, whose development roads are available to the public, there are now probably four thousand kilometers of hard-surface road in Venezuela, together with many subsidiary highways which can be used in dry seasons.

Over all these roads there is today a busy traffic of busses and trucks. These latter constitute a problem for the railroads which is almost as difficult as the engineering problems. Just as in the United States in the early days of motorized road vehicles, the trucks and busses have the advantage of highways that have been built and are maintained at practically no cost to the individual owners of this motorized transportation. These individual bus and truck owners are not responsible for accidents and other inevitable losses to anywhere near the extent of the railroads.

There are less than a thousand miles of railroads in all Venezuela.

In contemplating the building of further roads, the nation will doubtless take into consideration, not only the engineering difficulties, but the further deterrents that exist in the labor laws which so restrict railway operations as to make them generally unsuccessful financially in Venezuela today. These laws limit the hours of work, impose heavy burdens for injuries—actual or feigned—prevent layoffs, and so hamper the operations on the one end and increase the cost of operation on the other that, outside of small lines operating in the vicinity of Lake Maracaibo, there is hardly today a foot of railway in Venezuela that isn't losing money for its owners.

A new railway now under construction from El Palito to Palmasola will connect the Valencia–Puerto Cabello Railway with the Bolívar Railway.

The El Palito–Palmasola line passes through the valley of the Yaracuy, where good-quality bananas are grown and may be exported in fairly large quantities to the United States. The Venezuelan Banana Company, which is developing this business, has a capital of 2,000,000 bolivars, of which 1,000,000 bolivars was subscribed by the government through the Ministry of Agriculture.

The Venezuelan banana trade just now has difficult competition with the United Fruit Company, which is equipped with the most up-to-date machinery for handling bananas without damaging the fruit. Venezuela still lacks this mechanical competency in handling the fruit, so that her bananas frequently go into the world market bruised. In the standardization of perfect fruit in the export realm, this becomes a serious defect for a Number One classification. With the completion of the

El Palito–Palmasola line it is expected that these defects will be remedied.

The Andean region produces coffee, which is mostly exported through Maracaibo. Imported goods, machinery, textiles, and other supplies also come in through that port.

The La Ceiba Railroad runs from near Valera and Trujillo to Lake Maracaibo. Its length is eighty-one kilometers, gauge 3.6 feet. It is privately owned and makes money.

The El Vigia–Sta. Barbara Railroad takes products brought by highway from Mérida and Tovar to Sta. Barbara on the Escalante River and thence to Maracaibo. Length, sixty kilometers, 3.6-foot gauge. It is owned and operated by the government and covers its operating expenses. It is run down to some extent, and the government is considering spending some two million bolivars for the rehabilitation of this line.

The Táchira railroad runs from Táchira station to Encontrados, on the river Catatumbo and connects by river and lake to Maracaibo. It is privately owned and makes money. Length, 125 kilometers, 3.6 gauge. The Táchira station is the southern terminal of this railway, and is connected with San Cristóbal by highway.

All three of these railroads run from Lake Maracaibo (or navigable rivers emptying into the lake), across the flat country (subject to flooding), to the foot of the mountains, where they connect with the highways going back into the interior.

There have been proposals to extend the railways back into the mountains and to join them together, bringing them to a common port to be established at the foot (southerly end) of Lake Maracaibo. Recent investigation, however, rather indicates the improbability of any immediate action by the government along these lines.

*The Orinoco Valley.* There are two means of access to the llanos of the Orinoco from the central trunk line above referred to—one through San Juan de los Morros, the other from San Felipe, on the Bolívar Railway south towards Acarigua. Railroads through these passes have been talked of and proposed for many years for the purpose of bringing the cattle from the llanos to the central zone and the coast—cattle for the meat supply of the central zone, which requires about 125,000 head a year, and for export (through Puerto Cabello).

The export of beef was an important factor in Venezuela's economy some few years ago. But the cattle business is now bad, and cattle stocks are decreasing because there is no profit. The cattle must be driven to Maracay; the cost of driving and loss of weight is around fifty bolivars per head. After the drive the cattle are reconditioned for market in grass fields in the Aragua valley around Maracay.

According to public officials who have studied the problem, the proposed llanos railroad would avoid these losses, and the cheaper transport would insure some profit to cattle raisers. The railroad would obviate the need of fattening the cattle on the Maracay pastures, thus permitting the latter to be used for more intensive agricultural development and the raising of general food supplies for Caracas.

*The Central Railroad.* This line runs easterly and southerly from Caracas to Ocumare del Tuy. It has never paid (it has 4-per-cent gradients) and a few years ago it was abandoned by its owners, and was taken over and is now operated by the government. It has been proposed to extend this line.

Adequate railway facilities provided our country with fast, dependable, all-year-round bulk transportation and thus made readily available in any part of the nation or for export the products of every part of the nation, and in this way hurried and insured the rapid, successful settlement of the United States. These were then the only means of rapid transportation, as they preceded the era of automotive transport.

Those who built the railroads of the United States, in addition to giving incalculable help to the development of our natural resources and thereby tremendously increasing the wealth of the nation, also helped unify the people of a vast and varied area into a homogeneous whole. And they did all of this not as government officials using public money but as private citizens using private funds. It is true that our government units helped either with land or money grants or both, but the management and operation of the railroads in the

United States were kept in the field of private enterprise.

Before the coming of automotive competition and hard-surfaced roads, the United States needed all of its railroad mileage. Now it has perhaps much too much. Since Venezuela is practically virgin railway territory and her officials can determine the potential transportation value of automotive units, it should be possible for her to determine almost exactly how much more if any and what kind of railroad facilities she needs to forward her best economic development.

☆          ☆          ☆

Another transportation auxiliary of rapidly growing utility is the airplane. While it is comparatively a new service in Venezuela, it now covers the nation widely with trips which increase in frequency as the prosperity of the lines grows.

The facility of getting over Venezuela, which these lines provide, is an outstanding development in transportation.

For example, when I visited a mission near the headwaters of the Orinoco River, I asked the English-speaking medical director of the mission how often he got to Caracas. He reminded me that, if you use the ordinary modes of travel, it takes from two weeks to thirty days to make the journey by river and automobile, if you have good luck during the dry season. In the wet season, the trip is practically impossible.

"But," I said, "you can reach Caracas in less than a day by air."

"It costs over two hundred bolivars to reach it by airplane, and it is difficult to hoard that much money for travel in the upper waters of the Orinoco River," replied the director.

Nevertheless they are hoarding it, and the planes which reach that section, probably one every two weeks, are occupied to full capacity.

While I was in Venezuela the Aeropostal bought two fourteen-passenger planes to care for the increase in flying business. These are in addition to the six Lockheed high-speed passenger planes now in service. The government is also buying four large cargo planes for a freight service over the mountain distances.

The Aeropostal, as the government service is called, maintains at Maracay not only an up-to-date airfield, but also a school for pilots. This school collaborates with the military air service, providing an opportunity for the pilots trained by the army to secure work on the commercial lines.

Pilots are selected for the service according to their ability in flying. A co-pilot is chosen by the senior pilot from the army. A pilot receives 2,000 bolivars per month. The pilots are excellent, and the record of the Aeropostal on accidents will compare well with flying records anywhere.

In a land that seems able to pay high prices for its transportation, I am inclined to think the most immediately encouraging feature of the entire program is the rapid growth which is being made by aerial transportation.

The Pan American Airways maintains an excellent flying service from Miami, Florida, to Venezuela four days each week. One service goes direct to Maracaibo from Miami and makes the trip in about ten hours. The other service from Miami to La Guaira goes by way of Trinidad and makes stops at different West Indian ports. The planes are equipped with rubber lifeboats, rafts, collision mats, two weeks' food and water supply for each passenger, bedding, fishing tackle, etc.

# CHAPTER XXII

## *Maracaibo—A Modern City Which Began Life on Stilts*

---

WHEN THE PRIMEVAL PLOWMAN had finished tumbling the Andes Mountains from the ooze in western Venezuela, he left a basin between the Colombian Andes and that cordillera which takes its swing northeastward from the southwestern corner of Venezuela to the eastern coastal region. In the center of the basin, shaped like a huge bottle to be poured full from the Gulf of Maracaibo, is a lake several times bigger than the Sea of Galilee. From its narrow bottle neck to its bottom is a distance of 125 miles. In its widest bulge it is over seventy miles across.

Creation left the basin thus, a torrid, tropical region with this lake in the center. The coastal Indians built thatched huts on stilts in the shallower waters of the lake. It was natural for them to do this. The neighboring jungles were full of jaguars, pumas, tapirs and anteaters. It doubtless occurred to the Indians that a house on stilts in a lake would be safer than one located in the low, swampy lands of the jungle. So when a Spanish explorer, Alonso de Ojeda, in 1499 came upon Lake Maracaibo and found the Indians living in huts set on piles, paddling their dugouts from door to door, he was reminded of Venice and called the land Venezuela.

We wish Ojeda could come back and take a look at the city of Maracaibo now just to see what man in the last twenty years has done to improve upon nature. From a sleepy village in a swampy country, steaming under the heat of the tropics at sea level, Maracaibo has become a modern, industrial city with ice-cream sodas for sale at the drugstore and refrigerating plants which work all night in thousands of modern residences inhabited by people who know how to strike a proper balance for comfort, independent of the temperature.

I saw Lake Maracaibo from every angle; at night the electric lights from hundreds of oil derricks reflecting on a coast line of fifty miles looked like the electric display of a metropolis; in the daytime, as I approached the productive activities in a launch and saw these innumerable oil derricks emerging from the water, they looked, from a distance, like the naked trees of a burned-out forest. When I got to a point where I could step upon a catwalk that ran from one oil derrick to another, my impression was of an oil field that had fallen victim to a mammoth Mississippi flood which had set it afloat.

You realize two distinct facts about oil production in this basin. The field is geared to high volume. The cost of production is relatively so great that a slow result would not carry the enterprise. When the oil companies had been in business here apparently at full tilt for a dozen years, they were still obliged to import new capital for the development of the industry. Modern geology has given to the industry a measuring intelligence, so that in going after the reserves of the Maracaibo basin they have dared to expend an amount of capital which approaches the $500,000,000 mark.

I live in an oil field in the Mid-west where men carry on a perpetual debate upon the probability that more money has gone into the earth in search of oil than has come out in equivalent oil values. The only thing I felt sure about after I had studied the oil situation from a layman's viewpoint in Maracaibo was that nothing would have ever produced an oil field in Maracaibo except the generous expenditure of a capital that was not afraid to drill for oil under the water.

"How do you drill an oil well in fifty feet of water?" I asked my guide.

He began to answer the question by taking me aboard a fast motor speedboat. We reached an area where drilling was in progress. To get here we had threaded our way through four lanes of derricks connected by wooden catwalks; then there were eighteen more lanes out in the lake. These lanes were in lines straight as the crows can fly and stretched as far as I could see. The derricks further out were about six hundred meters apart. Reaching an area where drilling was in progress, my attention was called to a barge upon which was an immense crane. It picked up a cement pile 133 feet long, twenty-four inches square, and weighing forty tons, and put it in position above the water while a pile driver drove it down in fifty feet of water. A similar cement pile was driven at each corner of the location, and eight more to brace the corners and sustain the situation. Then, when the piles were set, a steel subbase for the derrick was set upon the piles and concreted in place. Rig builders began work upon a 122-foot derrick. I was told that a drilling barge would soon come alongside and in seventeen days complete the well.

On shore I was shown the Lago plant for constructing these forty-ton concrete piles. The forms for the cement are laid on great carriages mounted on wheels. The cement mixer empties into these dump cars, and when the pile is finished the carriage is run out on a track to the pile-driving barge in the lake. Only a small number of men are required to handle these giant monoliths.

On shore one is amazed with the immense scale on which everything is done. Each of the three companies operating in this field, the Lago, V.O.C. and Mene Grande, have enormous warehouses in which millions of dollars' worth of material is stored. Machine shops, woodworking shops, pump stations, commissaries are all built in impressive proportions. There is a constant stream of materials and supplies coming in and a constant stream of oil going out.

Locomotives, trucks, motorcars contribute to an increditable activity geared up to every kind of high-powered machinery.

Room has been found for tank farms required to handle 400,000 barrels of oil a day produced in this area. Farther away space has been found for attractive housing colonies, for both foreign and national employees. Clubs for employees, hospitals, schools, sports fields, all blend in this unexpected picture of activity, giving to the Maracaibo field a glamour which belongs to big things well done.

Once again in Venezuela I was impressed with the encouraging fact that the men who have charge of petroleum production possess a thorough knowledge of what they are doing and the broad human sympathies and character that enable them to do it.

I found the manager of the Lago Petroleum Corporation, when I visited Maracaibo, to be such a man— a genial man whose eyes can twinkle and whose energies seem limitless.

After graduating from the Colorado School of Mines as petroleum engineer, he rolled up his sleeves and started in on the ground floor as a driller. He then learned the tropics—going first to Mexico as petroleum engineer for the Pan-American interests and later to Venezuela as superintendent of production. In his present position he has charge of all operations for Lago.

Unfortunately, I arrived just too late to meet his predecessor, who after some thirty years in the tropics,

ten of them in charge of developing the great Lago
Fields, is now among the experienced officials who
apply the knowledge gained in the industry throughout the world to conducting Standard of New Jersey's
multitudinous activities from the nerve center of New
York City.

A man who placed me under many obligations at
Maracaibo was Mr Link, a member of the Lago staff
in charge of employees' welfare. I soon discovered his
obsession. At home he would be a member of the Board
of Education in charge of athletic activities. I was there
to talk about oil, so he started out by showing me the
public playgrounds, schoolhouses, pictures of athletic
events in which Venezuelan children were making the
welkin ring with something like North American enthusiasm.

Mr Link is a busy man at his regular tasks, and his
diversion would make a full-time job for a person less
gifted. In charge of the athletic program of Lago, he
showed me a dozen beautiful trophies of the program
for 1939. Silver mugs with golden linings, group figures
glorifying basketball, baseball, foot racing and other
expressions of sport marked the genuine enthusiasm
which the devotees of athletics have achieved in this
tropical zone.

Believing that the way to get closer to the common
interests among peoples is through these athletic activities, and having discovered sports to be the best
medium to bring youth together, he has organized the

first basketball court in this city of 150,000 people. He has established a typical baseball field with proper bleachers in a little spot overshadowed by oil derricks and the productive equipment of an oil field. An athletic organization for the state of Zulia, of which Maracaibo is the capital, has been launched under his leadership. They are now projecting a stadium for general athletics. It will cost $150,000, 60 per cent of which will come from the state of Zulia, 40 per cent from public contribution. It would be impossible to follow this logic and demonstration without realizing that he has found an important way to better health and social co-operation in Venezuela.

I spent a good deal of time observing the progress that has been made in sanitation, the very ample hospitalization for the petroleum colonies and the larger provisions now being made for a general hospital to be built by the government at a cost of 2,500,000 bolivars.

There is so much about sanitation and hospitalization in this book that the impression may prevail that I am overemotional on the subject. As a matter of fact, emotion plays a much smaller part in the building of hospitals here than does necessity. After oil was discovered, particularly in the jungle areas of Venezuela, it became apparent that if these fields were to be developed economically the question of health and sanitation would be the first problem facing the industry.

The long history of failure which preceded the construction of the Panama Canal demonstrated the fact that work in jungle areas cannot be successful without effective sanitation and medical supervision. That the United States recognized this fact and succeeded where France failed emphasizes the primary difference between the efforts of two countries on sanitation and health.

In all the areas in Venezuela where adequate medical service does not exist, the petroleum companies from the beginning have stressed not only healthful working conditions but complete medical care for their staff employees and laborers and their families. It was recognized that if a laborer's family was not enjoying good health, this would be reflected in the health of the employee. As a part of a business program, therefore, the company has constructed hospitals in all the main camps and in cities like Maracaibo, with every sort of first-aid and dispensary equipment in the outlying points of the fields.

The Dutch Shell hospital at Maracaibo has been described in one of the European medical journals as one of the largest and most beautiful in the tropics. It has a modern operating theater as well as all modern equipment for major operations. It also is equipped with the latest X-ray apparatus and diathermy machines, and its complete laboratory is equipped for making blood examinations and others necessary in the treatment of tropical diseases, and has at all times carried a competent medical staff. Upon visiting the hospital one is immediately impressed with the color scheme of the several rooms which has been designed to produce a very soothing effect.

In addition to the great hospital being projected by the government there are two additional outstanding federal projects. The new modern water-supply system, described in the chapter concerning water works, was the first of seventy new water-works systems to be installed in the larger cities of Venezuela under the Three Year Plan.

Another ambitious project contemplates the opening of the Maracaibo bar. Engineering talent is there making studies of the project under the direction of General Kuts, former Chief Engineer of the United States Army. It is understood that engineering judgment in regard to this project is divided. Some engineers declare the project to be feasible within the estimated cost, while others believe the cost will be far greater than estimated. Some question remains as to whether the large expenditure is economically desirable in view of the fact that the main traffic of Maracaibo, which is oil, is now cared for by a fleet of tankers created for shallow draft which do not need easement of the bar in their traffic. Very few freight boats of heavy draft come to Maracaibo. The Grace Line shifts its Maracaibo traffic into smaller boats at Curaçao. German and Dutch boats of shallow draft take fairly good care of general demand. Oil is by far the largest export, so the question as to whether the government will embark upon an expenditure of 60,000,000 bolivars for the removal of a bar which doesn't seriously impede the present situation remains undecided.

You leave Maracaibo with the impression that this, which is at once the most expensive and one of the most productive single oil fields in the world, offers an amazing cross section of that Western genius which successfully expresses itself wherever difficulties are to be overcome. That genius has taken from the earth and the waters under the earth more than a billion and a half barrels of crude oil in less than a quarter of a century. It has cured a population of sickness and sloth, taught it how to be modern and to prize sanitation and education. It has made known to this part of the world practically every industry which contributes to the comfort and convenience of human beings; it has kept this tropical region, once a pest hole, a place in which one may live with a fair degree of comfort and good health. It hasn't finished, but is working with a greater eagerness than has characterized it at any time in the past twenty years.

# CHAPTER XXIII

## *The Development of Oil Activities*

---

IN VENEZUELA the history of oil is very recent. In its main operations it is less than twenty-five years old. So far as foreign capital is concerned, it started out as a clean-cut gamble in a difficult and uncertain field requiring heavy investment. It is still gambling.

Exploring in eastern Venezuela, one petroleum company spent $30,000,000 before it developed a commercial oil field. A vital thing about the expenditure was that it opened a genuine field when it finally drilled into a strike.

An oil venture in Venezuela has of necessity been a big-business activity from the beginning. Although Venezuelan oil fields had produced 1,695,675,000 barrels of oil to the end of 1938, which is a little over 5 per cent of the crude oil produced throughout the world in all time, oil operations there started out in bad luck and discouragement.

A few incidental references in reports of early explorers to seepages of petroleum, and occasional allusions by Venezuelans to use of this substance, summarize the history of the industry in Venezuela before the latter part of the nineteenth century. In the year 1883 the Compañía Petróleo del Táchira, a Venezuelan organization, obtained from the state of Táchira a concession on a small tract of land near Rubio, about twenty-five kilometers from San Cristóbal. This concession permitted the owner to prospect for petroleum and allied substances, as well as to refine and sell such products. The supply of oil obtained on this concession had been secured from pits or wells dug by hand into the outcropping oil-bearing formations. This property is still being worked today.

No further interest was shown in petroleum until 1904, when a new mining code was enacted which contained special reference to petroleum and asphalt. The new mining code provided that claims could no longer be taken up by denouncement proceedings, but only under special contract entered into with the Federal Executive. This law was remodeled in 1905 and placed in the hands of the Executive a great deal of power which heretofore he had not possessed. And in 1906 an executive decree outlined the whole procedure under which concession contracts were to be entered into under the 1905 law. Many such concession contracts were made, and four of these are in force today, namely:

Colón district (Colón Development Co., Ltd.)
The Maracaibo and Bolívar district (Venezuelan Oil Concessions, Ltd.)

Buchivaco district (British Controlled Oilfields, Ltd.)
Silver and Zamora district (North Venezuelan Petroleum Co.,
  Ltd.)

One of these early concession contracts was entered
into with General Aranguren, a Venezuelan who had
discovered seepages of oil in the Maracaibo district and
attempted to develop the obvious fact that oil existed,
but failed because of the exhaustion of funds. This concession contract formed the basis for the Venezuelan
Oil Concessions, Ltd. It spent a great deal of money in
the districts of Maracaibo and Bolívar, which were
covered by the concession contract. The Royal Dutch
Shell, owned largely by British and Dutch capital,
came to the relief of the Venezuelan Oil Concessions.
It, in turn, was about to abandon the project after the
expenditure of large sums of money for test purposes.

In 1908 the Venezuelan Asphalt Company entered
into a concession contract to develop an asphalt field,
but this has not become an important part of Venezuelan endeavor, since asphalt deposits located elsewhere,
notably in Trinidad, had better transportation resources, lower labor costs and easy opportunity to reach
asphalt markets. Moreover the whole subject of crude
asphalt has been rendered unimportant by modern petroleum refining, which is producing asphalt as a by-
product at a cost less than that at which asphalt might
be mined from so-called asphalt lakes. The extensive
areas covered by the concession contract of the Venezuelan Asphalt Company were acquired by the Royal
Dutch Shell group.

Under the codes of 1909–10 a roving concession contract was entered into with Mr John Allen Tregelles, an Englishman, to explore the whole northern part of Venezuela. After a well near Cumaná was drilled without results, his rights lapsed after a period of two years through nonperformance.

The Venezuelan oil-concession contracts, until 1912, comprised large areas, usually entire districts, and were made on liberal terms. Large areas and liberal terms alone were able to attract necessary capital to explore and exploit because Venezuela had little geological information as a guide for the explorers. The oil companies themselves had to secure and assemble it. While considerable work has been done in this respect, the available Venezuelan geological information, even today, is in no way comparable to that of the United States, where the United States Geological Survey, oil-company operations for over three quarters of a century, and scientific papers and books combine to give those interested a complete and accurate background. This lack of geological information, coupled with the fact that oil was not being produced in modern commercial quantities until 1914, caused Venezuela to continue the program of making contracts covering extensive areas on liberal terms.

The year 1914 was a big one for Venezuela. In 1914 the Caribbean Petroleum Company brought in three producing wells in Mene Grande and one in Perija, state of Zulia. In 1914 Venezuelan Oil Concessions,

Ltd., brought in a producing well near Cabimas. And in 1914 the Colón Development Company struck oil near Rio de Oro.

These important discovery wells brought about modification in 1915 of the mining codes of 1909–10, which served to restrict somewhat the rights and privileges established under the earlier mining code. An immediate result was to slow down and shortly nearly stop completely the leasing of any more areas by the oil companies. In 1918 the government issued a regulatory decree somewhat liberating the interpretation applicable to oil. The flow of oil capital from Mexico to Venezuela and Colombia was stimulated by Mexico's effort to apply retroactively the provisions of its Constitution of 1917 nationalizing the subsoil. Geological investigations were unabated in 1919 in Venezuela and Colombia. Hardly had their activities in Colombia been launched when an exaggerated idea of the value of their prospective fields inspired Colombians to pass a restrictive law without adequate guarantees to capital. The oil companies, as a result, almost entirely withdrew from the Colombian fields, other than where the Tropical and Barco companies operated on the old large-area concessions, until Colombia recently modified her petroleum laws on a liberal basis.

In the meantime Venezuela gave serious consideration to new modification of her mining laws. Venezuelan aid and encouragement to the oil companies were perfectly timed in that they were offered during the period

when Mexico's efforts were most determined to confiscate foreign-owned oil properties.

As a further inducement to foreign capital Venezuela
again modified her petroleum law in 1922 and established a fair working basis. Subsequent modifications in
1925 and in 1928 maintained the same liberal, fair basis
but dealt more with detail of operation than with fundamental principles.

Many of the oil companies operating in Venezuela
acquired oil leases covering extensive areas during this
period, and some of them spent many millions of dollars in unsuccessful exploration work. Although the
exploratory work continued, the Venezuelan government did not enter into any new contract between 1929
and 1934. Beginning again in 1934 and until the petroleum law of 1938 contracts were entered into with
the government by several companies for exploration
and exploitation rights.

Interestingly enough, the new restrictive 1938 oil law
in Venezuela has slowed down exploratory work there
just as restrictive laws did earlier in Mexico. And just
as Venezuela's earlier liberal laws had encouraged oil
capital to go there from Mexico, so today Colombia,
through recently liberalized laws, is encouraging oil
capital to undertake exploratory work, which it is
doing. There is a boom now going on in exploratory
work and lease acquisition in Colombia.

In the meantime the peak of Venezuelan oil production is kept high by its momentum, just as happened in

Mexico, where, although restrictive efforts began in 1917, the high peak of production was not reached until 1921. During this four-year period capital was busily searching for new areas in other countries and preparing to migrate to countries where conditions were more favorable.

To the extent that the recently initiated exploratory boom in Colombia is successful, the oil produced there will compete with Venezuelan oil in world markets and then affect its available outlets and its price.

The approximate acreage holdings in Venezuela of the important operating companies reported for 1939 were as follows:

|  | Total Gross Acres |
|---|---|
| Standard Oil Company of Venezuela | 6,003,544 |
| Lago Petroleum Corporation | 1,152,599 |
| Dutch Shell Group | 5,611,607 |
| Mene Grande Oil Co. (Gulf) | 2,399,109 |
| Socony-Vacuum | 2,002,938 |
| Caracas Petroleum Corporation | 3,013,179 |
| Cia Consolidada (Sinclair) | 991,778 |
| Pantepec Group | 339,383 |
| Texas Co. of Venezuela | 337,545 |
| Atlantic Refining | 102,911 |
| Vimax Oil Company | 115,163 |
| Esperanza Petroleum Company | 179,062 |
| British Controlled Oilfields, Ltd. | 859,923 |
| North Venezuela Petroleum Co., Ltd. | 1,413,437 |
| Coro Petroleum Company | 58,383 |
| Cia "El Llano" | 310,143 |
| Dakota Oil & Transport | 1,270,243 |

Only a small percentage of the oil companies actively operating in Venezuela have been successful in developing commercial production. The Beacon Sun Oil Company was very active in Venezuela from 1922 to 1930, during which time it held up to 1,750,000 acres under concession contracts and drilled ten wildcat wells, all without success.

The Richmond Petroleum Company of Venezuela, subsidiary of the Standard Oil Company of California, has been active in search for Venezuelan reserves since 1924. Although it has spent rather large sums in this endeavor, it failed to encounter substantial quantities of oil.

In its beginning days in Venezuela the Standard Oil Company of New Jersey spent $20,000,000 drilling wells in what looked like favorable territory in western Venezuela without striking a commercial field. Engineers and geologists were working everywhere in the Maracaibo fields, which then held the center of attention and expectation so far as oil was concerned in Venezuela.

If the companies desire to retain the land for exploitation purposes, it is necessary that they make a thorough survey of the territory. First, the boundaries must be traversed with chain and transit, and permanent corner posts set with suitable reference ties. Rivers, roads and boundaries, both state and district, which fall within the limits or within a kilometer outside the limits, are also traversed.

The Minister of Fomento, at the end of the exploration period, requires that the lease owners submit to him for approval their large-scale maps of the entire area. These must contain all details of the survey, maps of each 500-hectare parcel, together with all notes and calculation sheets used during the survey. The technical staff of the Department of Fomento checks these and collects a tax for each map, then passes them on to the minister.

Under the concession contract, the lessor has the exclusive right to explore and exploit the area retained for a forty-year period. During this time an annual tax per hectare is collected on a graduating scale. Beginning at two bolivars, the tax often climbs to five bolivars and in some cases to eight.

A royalty is collected on oil production, either in oil or its value in gold. The charge is made at current world prices at the nation's discretion, and the production figures are checked at the wells by technically trained Venezuelan officials.

The terms governing the oil contracts have been regarded as good for the nation. In all my questioning in Venezuela, I never heard a criticism touching the dealing between the oil companies and the government.

The state of the oil industry in Venezuela does not seem to be challenged by any threat of confiscation, such as has ruined the oil situation in Mexico, surrendered to Communism, and in Bolivia, surrendered to the plainer type of common theft.

The Venezuelan oil industry has never been disturbed by the several changes in the oil law during the past years. However, the new legislation adopted in 1938 contains provisions so onerous that it is doubtful if any foreign company would now make application for a contract under it.

Lawyers both of the government and of the oil companies contend that the law contains unconstitutional provisions.

Some hint of an intention on the part of the government of Venezuela to go into the oil business itself, to exploit, refine and transport its own oil, is contained in Article Two of the new law, which provides that the government itself may exercise the right to develop, refine and transport petroleum, and that it may form government companies through which to do this.

The concession contracts that have been entered into heretofore, and cannot be abrogated by new laws, run for forty years. This means that the first ones still have something like twenty years to run, while many of them have practically the full period before them, since prior to the 1938 oil law additional contracts have been entered into continuously as the explorations have grown.

A concession contract in itself, regarded by laymen as some sort of glamorous possession acquired by foreign capital, is a vested property right under which the holder may gamble on the advice of his geologists, with the government sharing in the benefits but not in the losses.

Many millions of dollars have been invested in areas which have yielded nothing. The capital expenditure of the oil companies in Venezuela each year is staggering; for the year 1939 it is estimated it was $50,000,-000. This is outside of money spent on royalties, wages or current expenses. It is for the permanent improvement and equipment of the fields.

All the petroleum laws have prohibited doing work in streets, plazas, private homes and gardens, even within the area governed by the concession contract. Article 13 of the new law retains this provision as far as the concessionaire is concerned, but apparently opens the door for the government to step inside the concession area and develop these zones to the exclusion of the right of the concessionaire.

The President of the Republic, in a recent address, spoke of the advisability that the nation should build a national refinery to produce its own oil products. However, the prerequisites for constructing the refinery, namely, the necessity of providing a regular outlet for crude oil and the assurance of adequate petroleum products in time of war, are lacking in Venezuela; and refineries have not been lucrative during the past several years.

For several years the Shell interests have operated a moderate-sized refinery at San Lorenzo. A modern one is now being built at Caripito by the Standard Oil Company, where it will take care of the growing production of the comparatively new fields of eastern Venezuela.

A new refinery in western Venezuela is being completed by Lago Petroleum Corporation at La Salina.

The oil refining for the great Maracaibo basin has, for the most part, been done at the Dutch islands of Aruba and Curaçao. Doubtless some advantages to the oil companies exist in having their main refining operation in these Dutch islands which have absolute free trade.

Most of the oil is taken to these islands by a fleet of eighty shallow-draft boats. The ownership of these boats is divided between the Dutch Shell, which owns forty of them, and the American companies, which own forty. Altogether twenty-four of these boats daily carry an average cargo of 17,000 barrels of oil, or a total delivery of 408,000 barrels per day, to the refineries in the Dutch islands. The remainder of the oil goes as crude to other world markets.

No one can visit Aruba, home of the Standard Oil refinery, without feeling that the presence of such a large refinery upon a coral reef in the Caribbean Sea is almost as inexplicable as is a coral reef.

Aruba was selected for physical and economic reasons to be the base of Lago Oil and Transport Company's refining operations. It has fine harbors and is only a few miles from the Maracaibo basin, and as already mentioned it is a land without a tariff wall in the Caribbean. Lago, to build its refinery, brought in some sixty million dollars' worth of equipment through an open market. It imports the living supplies for a large population without stopping to talk to the customs official. In a dozen years it has developed a population approaching eight thousand, made up of experts from the oil-conscious centers of the United States, scattered from Pennsylvania and New Jersey to California, through Ohio, Kansas, Oklahoma and Texas. We hear little of Aruba in the United States, but they know of her in Europe, to which she guarantees a never-failing supply of refined oil. The day I visited this remarkable spot the harbor was full of foreign tankers loading with oil for ports all over the world except the United States. Great Britain is the best customer Aruba possesses.

# CHAPTER XXIV

# *Oil Labor in Venezuela*

---

O IL LABOR IN VENEZUELA enjoys a status comparable to that of workers anywhere else in the world. Credit for this enviable attainment goes partly to a labor law which, while liberal even by American standards during the past several years, is considered—with one or two important exceptions—a generally fair and constructive piece of legislation. But I found more than a law, I found a spirit. The "why" of favorable labor conditions can be traced chiefly to an unusual spirit of cooperation between workers and management.

The root of the oil companies' labor policy is that increased earning capacity and improved living conditions depend on the industry's prosperity as well as the individual's growing skill at his trade. Every one of the numerous benefits enjoyed by oil workers, and there are many, has been adopted as a matter of good business and not out of philanthropy.

The situation as to the Venezuelan oil driller, which I have touched upon in my chapter about Caripito (Chapter XXV), I found to be typical of the general situation in all Venezuela. There are no longer any foreign drillers employed in the field except for very difficult exploration work. A driller has the highest skilled job in the oil fields. The minimum wage for unskilled labor is $2.66 per day, which is higher than the rate established by the Wage and Hour Law in the United States. A large number of workers in the skilled class get double this, and drillers receive about three times the amount. The wages paid in the oil fields are much higher than those paid by other industries in Venezuela.

On top of wages, oil companies are now required by law to provide housing, schools and medical attention for employees; as a matter of fact some companies have been doing this on their own initiative for ten years or more.

Originally houses were constructed by the companies in isolated areas in order to set an example of better housing and to improve the sanitary and living conditions of employees. Swamps were drained, mosquito-breeding streams sprayed, pure water supply and sanitary facilities provided. In neighboring public villages the companies frequently lent a hand in providing more healthful living conditions. The outside observer may well question whether this program may not have been carried too far. Human nature being what it is, there is a disposition in some quarters to look on the oil industry as a sort of Santa Claus with a bottomless sack. Be that as it may, the sanitary, medical and housing accomplishments of the oil industry in the jungles make an inspiring story—comparable to fighting yellow fever and malaria in the construction of the Panama Canal. In some sections of the country the hospitals in the oil camps are the only ones available, and the company doctors treat patients from the villages as well as employees and their families.

There is another phase of the labor law, which had gone into effect only recently and whose merits were much discussed while I was in Venezuela. I refer to its profit-sharing provisions. In simple terms these require the larger industries (meaning the oil companies), with few exceptions, to distribute from their profits each year up to 16 2/3 per cent of the pay roll. For smaller industries the tax is graded downward. The system has its defenders, especially among the workers. But its critics point out that such a lump-sum distribution of cash has tendency to dissipate wealth for a limited period, usually for nonconstructive purposes, because the human tendency when a windfall occurs is to blow everything on one spree. There is no lasting contribution to the country's purchasing power, it is argued, and employees are in no way aided in accumulating a backlog of savings.

Some idea of the extent of the working of the profit-sharing plan might be gained from the fact that last year the oil companies paid out to labor ten million extra dollars, which was supposed to represent the share of labor's profits. In a number of cases, however, it represented the oil companies' belief that it was desirable to go along with the law, because in some instances the 12½ per cent of the wages paid out did not represent profits.

I find that the oil companies themselves lean toward the so-called Plan for Savings, which was made effective before political agitation forced inclusion of the profit-sharing feature in the labor law.

In one company, the Plan for Savings provides for a voluntary contribution by an employee of from 3 to 10 per cent of his current wages. To these deposits the company adds fifty cents on the dollar, plus an annual provisional contribution. The funds are placed in the hands of trustees, and the employee has the option of investing in Venezuelan government bonds or in accordance with further options which may be worked out. Each year he may withdraw a certain proportion, but the majority remains on deposit to aid him in accumulating a small estate. In case an employee leaves the company or dies, everything standing to his credit— both his own deposits and those of the company—is returned to him or his survivors.

It is reasonable to suppose that when a worker has saved some money, owns property, and therefore has an interest in perpetuating the economic system of the country, he is a stabilizing influence in his community.

There is no question but that most of the cash distributed in the profit-sharing provision of the labor law is estimated to have been spent in celebrating, whereas reports on the Plan for Savings showed that in some areas 90 per cent of the participants did not withdraw any of their savings and the company deposits, but left the entire amount in the fund.

Helping the worker who is willing to help himself is sound philosophy.

A further example of this is found in the mutual sickness benefits and group life-insurance plans that have been developed in some oil communities.

Employee contributions in the mutual sickness-benefit plan are matched dollar for dollar by the companies, and in the group life-insurance plan the company bears half the cost. An interesting feature of the sickness-benefit plan is that, in addition to being mutual, it is organized on a strictly local basis. This has the valuable advantage of bringing the pressure of fellow employees to bear on any worker who might be tempted to take a little vacation beyond the normal convalescent period for his illness.

The history of collective bargaining in Venezuela is an interesting one.

There are unions in the oil fields (or syndicates, as they are known) as elsewhere in Venezuela. Their rights are strictly defined by law—but so are their limitations. When syndicate leaders are found to be using their organization's influence for political purposes in-

stead of for the benefit of the workers in smoothing out
any differences between employer and employees, the
government cracks down.

This provision was the outgrowth of political activity during the early stages of union organization in
Venezuela. When the law of public order was passed
in 1936, professional syndicate labor leaders carried on
an aggressive campaign against the bill, and prior to its
passage called a general protest strike. In certain union
activities during the intervening years, as in the general
strike in 1936, observers have detected the obvious influence of radical Mexican labor leaders.

Students of labor relations describe four types of
employer-employee relationship—the autocratic, militant, co-operative and legislative.

While the oil industry in Venezuela experienced
some of the militant type of relations in the early activities of the petroleum syndicates, and the legislative type
in some of the provisions of the labor law, labor relations in the oil industry generally fall into the third,
or co-operative, group, in which the workers deal with
the management directly or through representatives of
their own choosing. As a result of these talks, which
impress me as being along lines of mutual co-operation
rather than mutual antagonism, a number of improvements in labor policy, as well as certain wage adjust-
ments, have been worked out. Some of the more important labor practices followed by most of the oil
companies might be summarized as follows:

(1) Fair and just treatment for all employees, with individual or collective dealing on a co-operative basis.

(2) A definite procedure for speedy adjustment of grievances without fear of discrimination for having raised the question.

(3) No discrimination against an employee on account of membership or nonmembership in any church, society, fraternity or union.

(4) Hiring and promotion solely on the basis of the employee's ability to do his job and his willingness to abide by the rules of the company.

(5) Protection of each employee against losing his job by limiting discharge only to serious infractions of the posted company rules; warning notice in writing in all other disciplinary cases before discharge.

(6) At least the prevailing scale of wages for similar work in the area.

(7) Eight-hour day.

(8) Safe and sanitary working conditions.

(9) Equal treatment for those doing similar classes of work.

(10) Opportunity for special training to qualify employees for better jobs.

(11) Development of an effective housing program for workers.

(12) Co-operation with employees for sports, social activities and development of mutual plans for social security.

As part of the program for promoting greater understanding between management and workers, and also to stimulate the latter's interest in doing better work, a system of individual progress reports has been worked out in some areas by management and employee representatives.

A progress report is really a sort of periodic inventory of the worker's assets. By means of regular personal interviews with each man on the pay roll and special ability rating cards, the management has a written record of each worker, and the man stands on his record; furthermore, employees have a right to check up periodically on their abilities and shortcomings. It is an excellent system.

I mentioned earlier a provision of the labor law requiring companies in isolated regions to provide schools. In the case of the oil industry the rule was largely superfluous.

"Going to school" in an oil camp is by no means confined to children of the workers. All workers receive job training, and in this manner Venezuelan artisans have been developed in every oil-field trade, including the highly skilled and technical job of drilling. For older boys trade schools and manual training are now under consideration. Foreman conferences are conducted regularly to train men in responsible leadership.

Recognizing that friendly understanding between Venezuelans and foreigners was impossible as long as the language barrier stood in the way, the oil companies have arranged for Spanish instruction in the various camps, and at the present time practically all foreign employees who do not already speak the language, as well as many members of their families, are taking an intensive course in Spanish. For the most part the employee does this on company time.

The government, too, has recognized the value of education among the laboring classes. In visiting one of the government hospitals under construction I encountered a schoolroom for the instruction of workers in primary education. I was told that this is a feature on every public job in Venezuela. A place is fitted up

A Robert Yarnall Richie photograph from "World Petroleum"

Producing oil from shallow water just offshore from Lagunillas.

with benches where, for two hours each day, teachers give instruction to the workers in pursuance of the campaign to reduce illiteracy. At first the workers didn't care much about it and gave poor co-operation, but today there is a rivalry among them as they compete for grades.

I was told by one of the teachers that definite progress in adult primary work is being made by this plan all over Venezuela today. The instruction is, of course, of the simplest type, much of it being oral. It is a part of the government's plan to wipe out illiteracy in Venezuela in five years. Since there are probably something over thirty thousand common workers on government improvements just now, this becomes really an educational movement of major importance.

At the moment, the oil industry in Venezuela has no major labor problems. This is true very largely because of the growing tendency of management, labor and the government to recognize as the first principle that the welfare of labor and management is dependent on the prosperity of the industry in which they both are engaged. The situation is a haven compared to Mexico, where the laborer stands in confused and unrequited idleness amidst the industrial bankruptcy his radical leaders have brought upon him.

# CHAPTER XXV

## *An Oil Camp—Caripito*

WHEN A Standard Oil representative invited me to spend a week end in the "oil camp" at Caripito, I accepted with a feeling that probably I would not have a very comfortable visit. The idea of living in a camp in a tropical interior of Venezuela didn't seem alluring, but I wanted to see this particular camp. It is the headquarters for the new Standard Oil development of eastern Venezuela.

At Quiriquire, the Standard has developed a major field. Already the production is thought to have reached its peak at seventy-two thousand barrels a day. Caripito, a few miles away, is on the Rio San Juan, which provides a transportational outlet to the Gulf of Paria on the Caribbean.

In another location near El Tigre, 110 miles southwest, the Gulf Corporation, called the Mene Grande in Venezuela, has developed the Oficina field.

These two operations have excited Venezuela with

the prophecy that someday the developments in eastern Venezuela will equal, if not eclipse, the production of the Maracaibo basin in western Venezuela.

Mrs Allen and I started from La Guaira in a Standard Oil airplane, a Lockheed, piloted by an aviator with an international reputation, who is called Jerry by every man in the Standard organization.

The plane flew east over the blue waters of the Caribbean, giving us a view of the entrancing coast line with its rugged Andean background. We saw from an aerial distance the new Mene Grande works at Barcelona and Puerto la Cruz, where important transportational and dockage facilities are being created. Then we turned southward from the sea, climbed a mountain or two across the eastern vertebrae of the Andes, and began to drop into an attractive valley where there wasn't a man-made thing in sight except a large tin-roofed shed and a stack of gasoline drums. We were going to land there.

I kept looking for the tents of the oil camp. Having read all the snake stories in modern South American literature, I wondered how the tents were protected against reptilian life.

We were ushered into an automobile and taken twenty miles over an oiled road built by Standard. Still I didn't see any tents.

We climbed a hill and arrived unexpectedly at a beautifully located residential town, which had not been visible from the tree-enshrouded road. It looked like a country-club suburb in the United States. An

attractive golf course, modern houses, many of which
had a new, streamlined finish to them, green undulating
lawns, glorious flowering shrubbery, tropical fruit trees,
well-laid-out drives and sidewalks, a new church, a
large hospital on a neighboring hill, a big commissary
building, a group of modern offices set in the midst of
tropical landscaping, a clubhouse with wide-open
doors, windows and a veranda made an amazing
picture.

During the ride from the airfield the road had cut
through a dense tropical jungle, where we stopped to
look at the various types of native birds seen in the tree-
tops. We even caught a glimpse of a monkey.

We had been so far away from a modern country-
club district that I was altogether unprepared for the
surprising spectacle.

"What town is this?" I asked Mr H. R. Barbour.

"This is the Caripito camp," said he.

And so I discovered that an "oil camp" in Venezuela
is a place where you do not camp out.

In addition to the many attractive houses occupied
by the staff and office personnel of the Standard Oil
Company, there were, over the brow of the hill, hundreds of smaller houses built for occupation by the oil
workers. These were all modern homes with pure running water and electric lights.

Near by was the village which had been there for a
great many years, but which had undergone rapid expansion following the neighboring oil development. It

furnished a contrast in the methods of living on the part of the old residents and those adopted for oil workers under the Standard Oil provisions.

Some of the oil workers still live in the old village. A worker is given an additional bolivar a day if the company has not yet furnished him with quarters. Some of the workers do not like modern houses. They have to be taught how to use the bath and toilet facilities.

However, this old village is catching something from the oil camp. It was cleaner and in much better repair than any of its kind I'd seen elsewhere in Venezuela. The Standard had run a water line from its filtration plant through the town. At a convenient place in the street a fountain was delivering free water. A line of people with empty five-gallon gasoline cans waited their turn at the fountain. When I called attention to this popular use of the repossessed gasoline can, a member of the party turned philosopher.

"This empty gasoline can," said he, "is another step toward civilization. It makes better roofing than grass thatching because it keeps out both water and vermin. As a utensil it is sought after because it is more sanitary than the old calabash container whose porous sides, the water engineers tell us, collecting germs of disease continually, add peril to health. The gasoline can is a household utensil, even a bathtub for the baby. When it gets leaky they use it on the roof. The gasoline can is not a mark of poverty in Venezuela. It is proof of affluence and a forerunner of the more abundant life."

The more I visited about the main headquarters at Caripito the more my information grew as to what an "oil camp" is in all its component parts.

Mrs Allen and I went to the guest house, a commodious, homelike place, with private bath for every room, electric fans, wide windows and a big living room. On the trees outside were the richest gifts of the tropics in flowers and fruits.

The first evening the petroleum hosts gave us a buffet dinner, to which over a hundred women and men living at the camp came to ask about home and tell us about Venezuela. There were many young engineers, geologists, geophysicists and chemists mixed in with the administrative members of the staff. I met a half-dozen young men whom I had known in Kansas and Oklahoma who had dropped from my ken after their graduation from the state university and other schools, only to turn up amongst the unexpected miracles of the evening.

The personnel of this camp told a story to justify the American faith in technical education as well as in the developing qualities of rugged backgrounds. I could have chosen from the membership of the camp men with practical efficiency and engineering capacities sufficient to run a major railroad system. I could have picked, from the graduates of the various universities and technical schools represented in the group, an outstanding faculty for a modern technical college. I could have selected from the administrative leaders, who have solved the problems that have challenged them in this difficult country, men gifted to run a successful government. It was a trained, proven crowd of administrators and assistants, all of whom had fought their way through the various avenues of the widely diversified service to their own position of importance, in a group that collectively must have been proud of themselves and individually of each other.

You get the hopes and dreams of people living in a group like this by listening to the things they talk about. The men and women in this crowd of over a hundred people spend their lives with the problems that grow up around oil production. They didn't seem to have any "small talk." They had radios, and therefore possessed a sketchy knowledge of the progress of the world. They generally listened to the Ford hour on Sunday evening. The latest styles of the well-dressed women went back to the last seasonal vacation in the United States.

I listened to the general manager and his assistants in charge of operations in the Quiriquire field in a general conversation. I was anxious for a glimpse of what they would talk about during a social evening at this oil camp. They were too far away from the United States to be familiar with the daily grist of New Deal propaganda; they were not close enough to the stock-market's centers to catch its vibrations; the nervous tension of Europe was not upon them directly; they hadn't been to any modern shows. They were talking about the improvement in the living conditions of the Venezuelan people at the camp and in improving the productive capacities of the workmen themselves. They were mentioning individual Venezuelans, some of whom had started as humble workers, who were making progress in engineering, drilling, driving a tractor, making brick or working at general construction activities. In simple language, they were gossiping about the help in a most humane and friendly tone.

Throughout the whole evening, wherever I listened to people, the theme generally touched the Venezuelan workers and the successful way the workmen were making a place for themselves in that camp. Only they didn't call it a social program. They didn't have any technical name for it. It was the daily reflection of their chief endeavor, which is to make more effective and mutual the interests which flow between the industrial administrators and the people.

After the dinner and the social hour which followed it, we all went over to the country club, where the weekly dance was in progress. While the dance was on, a United States wife, known as the "dean of women" in the camp because she had lived there longer than any other woman, circulated among the people and reminded them that a missionary was to provide a church service the next morning, which would be Easter.

After the service I had a visit with the missionary, Mr Turner, who had come here twenty years ago and was in charge of a mission station in the Caribe valley, where life was still very simple and thrived on primitive methods of producing coffee, cocoa and bananas. His experience had given him a very fine basis for his hope in the progress of the prevailing human type, the Indian and the Spanish mestizo.

He was enthusiastic over the fact that a good many hundreds of Venezuelans were joining his mission and getting interested in his program of Christian education and individual responsibility. He was somewhat the emotional type, of which Christian martyrs are re-cruited, but his experience had made of him a realist in results. He said the best contribution being made in this part of Venezuela came from the co-operation of the petroleum companies in sanitation and medicine, which, under the enlarged program, was reaching the general population.

Living close together, those who are here are chal-lenged by tests which eliminate them if they lack the qualities necessary for effective membership in a highly selective society. The members of the staff and their wives must blend with the situation. They must be highly responsive to the group obligations, which call upon every member for a high degree of tact and self-control.

It was somewhat astonishing to me that the effect of living in an atmosphere where the workers need many humane considerations from the bosses has developed the most practical social-service consciousness I've seen

anywhere in the world. In a very high sense, the men
who administer these extensive headquarters study how
to improve the intelligence, productivity, health and
contentment of the Venezuelan workers on the pay roll.

The administrators in every oil camp I visited took
me first to see the workers' modern houses. They pointed
out with pride the up-to-the-minute equipment in the
kitchens, the bathrooms, the screens upon the windows,
the water-filtration system, and all the scientific installation which, in one sweeping operation, have brought
the easygoing tropical zone into the sterner, cleaner
discipline of the temperate zone in its most finished
state.

These administrators also want you to realize the
proclivities of the present. The whole attitude is to increase, in every department, the number of efficient
Venezuelans and the work being performed by these
men. The administrators are training geologists and engineers among the better-educated Venezuelan men;
stenographers and accountants among the women who
have the qualifications. They are running a language
school in which the Americans study Spanish and the
Venezuelans study English.

The oil companies several years ago adopted a policy
of sending promising young Venezuelans to the United
States to finish their engineering education in the oil
fields and technical schools there. This policy of sending
educated Venezuelan young men to the States for a sort
of finishing course has worked well. They get back to

the oil camp with a viewpoint of added value to themselves and their country. When a young man comes back to Venezuela with the engineering education which the oil company has sent him to acquire, he begins to work at a salary of 800 bolivars a month ($250 in our money), plus board and room. He is under no contractual obligation to stay with the oil company. The fact is made perfectly clear, when he goes to the States, that he will be free to use his education in any way he chooses when he gets back.

When a Venezuelan is raised from $2.66 a day as a common worker to eight dollars a day as a driller, he gets full driller's wages.

"I swear by these Venezuelan well diggers," said R. B. Kester, the superintendent at Quiriquire, who took me into a jungle to watch them working on a well that was going down thirty-four hundred feet. "We let out most foreign drillers three years ago.

"All settled fields are now using Venezuelan drillers. They work efficiently, don't start arguments over incidental labor points, work eight hours a day, get twenty-five bolivars—about eight dollars—a day, and this, with free housing and other benefits, makes the driller really a ten-dollar-a-day man. He's satisfied. No such wages are paid in any other industry, and in addition his health and that of his family is safeguarded from tropical scourges by scientific sanitation and purified water.

"We still employ a few foreign drillers in the wildcat fields.

"As rapidly as possible we are breaking Venezuelans in as foremen. Once we were obliged to use 120 foreign foremen in Caripito. In four years we've cut it down to thirty-five. All the others are Venezuelans.

"Today, in any job for which we've trained him, I'd rather have a Venezuelan than a foreigner. We are developing them into welders and lathe men and to fill other jobs in pipe-line work formerly held by foreign labor.

"All caterpillar tractors and graders now are operated by Venezuelans. Formerly foreign labor had to be used because of the semiskilled nature of the work."

Mr Kester painted a vivid picture of the change that has come over the Venezuelan worker in a few years. "When I first came here," he said, "the Venezuelan laborer came to work with a banana and a piece of cassava. Now he has a well-filled dinner pail, with meat every day.

"When the operation started in this field," he continued, "it was difficult to get native Venezuelans for responsible work. There didn't seem to be any distinctive types that could be made subforemen. All the men were underfed, unresponsive; most of them had some fever, many had hookworm, and their efforts were feeble. Now they do twice as much work, and they all want to be corporals in the organization."

Accidents have been cut down. Last year there was only one accident in the transport division.

The turnover of labor is 65 per cent. Those who leave

the oil companies find that their added capacity to do the things they have learned at an oil camp sets them apart as superior workers in their communities. I verified this one day by talking to a ferryman who was doing an expert job running a boat on the Rio San Juan. He told me he acquired his mechanical skill in the oil camp. Thus the countryside is filling up with men with some advanced training who turn their greater competency into added opportunities for making money in a country suffering from a shortage of skilled labor.

The oil companies are emphasizing the importance of education to Venezuelans of the oil industry. The children of the workmen are encouraged to go into the service. All promotions in the service are given to men who have come up through the ranks; some of the older workers in line for jobs that require the ability to take care of the educational demands of a foreman's job need special concessions.

I saw an old-time worker who didn't have the qualifications to meet the new educational demands of his foreman job. He couldn't keep the drilling records required. So the company appointed a member of the drilling crew who could read and write to act as secretary for the old worker, whose years of service, as well as general ability as a driller, entitled him to the foreman job. He is probably the only driller foreman in the world with a personal secretary.

The humanly gratifying thing is the really friendly relationship which grows up between the company and the workers. Said one of the workers in the drilling field: "I find that if I treat these men right, they always respond."

The turnover in labor is decreasing as the improved housing situation becomes better understood. The reluctance of a certain portion of the workers to leave their old huts for new housings has passed away. Now the situation is rapidly reversing. Thousands who didn't know what electricity is are charmed with it. Many who didn't know what money is for, didn't know how to spend it and took no interest in the money angle of their jobs, now are up to the minute on the subject.

As I listened to the members of the executive staffs talk about their work, I was sharply conscious that their problems had more to do with the labor, housing and educational angles than anything else.

Engineering, mechanical and administrative skill has solved most of the problems of production, refining and marketing. The main problems of this great camp concerned the personnel, and the genuine interest of every staff member in these people provided the antithesis of indifference.

That's the spirit of the oil companies toward their Venezuelan workers.

# CHAPTER XXVI

## Dr Weiss of Quiriquire

---

Dr FRANZ XAVIER WEISS, who runs the Standard Oil
Company's hospital at Quiriquire, is an outstanding
authority on tropical diseases.

An Austrian by birth and education, now a Venezuelan citizen, he came to the Standard service with a background of superior experience to take over the difficult
health problem. At Quiriquire the petroleum company
had started to open an oil field in the heart of a jungle. Its
geologists and engineers had fought pests, reptiles and
fevers to explore the place. The company had spent
many millions to verify the explorations of its scientists
and get ready for a major operation. The success that
came finally has marked it in the oil world as a tri-
umphant achievement of man over nature.

The Standard knew that one of its difficulties in this
field would be with local labor already half sick from
years of neglect and underfeeding in an atmosphere
reeking with malarial poisons. Added to that problem

was the need of keeping imported labor of the company from falling victim to tropical maladies.

Today when you visit the oil camp and observe the clean and attractive spot the engineers have made on high ground that overlooks the neighboring jungle, the difficulties through which they have cut their way do not seem real. Surrounded by these well-built modern houses—comfortable dormitories, for the foreign personnel, and the perfectly kept group of new homes for the workers—it is difficult to visualize that they have lived lives of danger. By looking from the hill into the dense growth, above which now and then you catch the projection of an oil derrick, you know they've conquered a bad spot in the tropics.

I visited the hospital, with its green, clean lawn, its restful, spreading pavilions with their protective blinds and awnings. But it is only when you go inside and talk with the grave Dr Weiss that you sense the fact that a winning fight is being waged that may someday be traditional wherever scientists talk of men against the jungle.

Dr Weiss spoke of the healing effect which cleaner houses, pure water and watchful care are having upon the situation, now safely in hand. Here, in this spot that must have been the sickest, he gave me the most hopeful feeling about the tropical maladies.

When I asked him about syphilis, which is generally the most talked-of disease, he said that the estimates of the lay newspaper and magazine writers are far too high.

"I've seen it placed at 80 per cent," said he. "That's nonsense. I've studied it for fifteen years in this country. The percentage of those afflicted by it is never over forty. It is now probably little larger than 30 per cent.

"Don't forget that South America is not the only land afflicted by this scourge. All countries which allow prostitution suffer largely from the infection."

He said the Venezuelans' attack upon syphilis as well as upon the other venereal diseases would be helped by the fight they are now making against prostitution.

He made an interesting observation about the ravages of syphilis. Said he: "Through years of practice I have learned to let the arrested cases alone. Nature sometimes provides an immunity which protects the patient. I have learned to doctor symptoms and let arrested cases go. All over the world today, where this fight against syphilis is growing, there will be some unfortunate results from bad clinics which do not have enough faith in nature's immunities. They will make active arrested cases which should be let alone."

He spoke of the need of country hospitals in Venezuela and praised the activity of the new government in giving recognition to this grave necessity. He approved the intention of the government to require, hereafter, a period of country practice as a part of the legitimate training of every new doctor.

"All the tropical diseases are easy of cure," said he, "if they are not neglected. The hookworm need not be an incurable problem in any country. There is a high natural immunity in most of Venezuela against typhoid which prevents it from becoming epidemic.

"Malaria is the scourge, and the first line of attack is proper sanitation. The early recognition which these petroleum companies gave to this fact has made the oil camps the most healthful spots in Venezuela."

# CHAPTER XXVII

## *Ciudad Bolívar and Oficina*

---

A<small>T</small> CIUDAD BOLÍVAR, an interesting old city on the Orinoco, Dr Ovidio Parez-Agreda, the president of the state of Bolívar, was waiting to show me things when I arrived one day at the airport. Incidentally, the airport was established a decade ago but is undergoing reconstruction. It is to be a new model. It will take care of the necessities both of commercial and army air activities.

The president took me first to see the new government building, which was to be ready for occupancy in a month. It is a model of good taste and substantial construction. Then he showed me the site for the president's new residence, upon which work was already being started.

After that, he got down to business and showed me the new public market, new parks, new hospitals, and the foundation for the new packing plant. He offered to take me up the river and show me the intake where the new water works was to get its supply, and which was already about half finished. I took his word for that. He didn't have to show me the torn-up streets where water pipes were to be installed.

Then he took me in his automobile to see the highway being constructed to the gold fields—from Ciudad Bolívar to Tumeremo. It will go straight to the gold fields, which in 1937 produced 38,514,626 bolivars in gold. The highway will be 256 kilometers in length, of which about 70 kilometers of it were then completed. A branch highway may be built to the iron deposits which the Bethlehem Steel Company is now exploring to determine whether, under transportation difficulties, it can make a profitable development of the large ore deposit upon which it has a lease.

A well-known New York engineer, Mr Fred Lavis, who was retained by the Ministry of Public Works as adviser on matters relating to the general development of land transportation in Venezuela, has been surveying the possibility of a railroad from the Orinoco River to the ore deposits to connect them with water transportation. It isn't believed that he is going to advise the building of the railroad, owing to the growth of highway transportation and the sparseness of general tonnage along the route of the proposed line. In the analysis of the railway and highway situation in Venezuela, I am indebted to Mr Lavis for valuable information.

The president drove me over the entire span of the new highway. The road work was a queer mingling of modern and ancient methods. At one point the president stopped to show me the workmen heating the rock and cracking it by this ancient method, best known to the Venezuelan worker. Elsewhere they were using dynamite and modern road-building machinery. But everywhere, whether modern or ancient methods were in use, they were making speed.

Along the way we stopped at a well-organized labor camp, where a large crowd of workers were comfortably established. At a near-by residence I met the director of the work, Dr Delgado, an able young Venezuelan who was graduated from Stanford University, and who was enthusiastic over the progress the job was making.

The common laborer gets the equivalent of $1.50 a day, but so much of the labor is expert, such as blasting, driving grading machines, trucks, tractors, etc., that the average labor wage on the job is very much higher than this.

The road is to be rock-ballasted, and eventually will have a top dressing of asphaltic oil.

On the way back to town, as we were driving through the twilight, the president, who spoke English fluently, said, "I did a good job today. I ordered 274,000 bolivars expended on public works."

When I called attention to the fact that it was a substantial sum for one day's expenditure, he explained that it covered a variety of purposes, including work on the new public market, the new slaughter plant, the new hospital, and the draining of a lagoon to turn a malaria swamp into producing land.

The president talked of many hopeful indications. Owing to modern attention to the fish industry, people were eating more fish than they had eaten before, much more than in most places. Fish was both abundant and cheap: two and a half kilos, two and a half cents in bolivar value, or practically one cent a pound. The president is hurrying a plant for the processing of fish to ease the general food situation.

Improved handling of meat has increased consumption of beef to a point where it is nearly three times per person greater than in Caracas.

Our conversation threw a hopeful light upon the difficult food situation, and was the more encouraging because it indicated a healthy rivalry now going on among the presidents of the various states to improve the local production of food supplies in the way of fish, vegetables, poultry and citrus fruits.

In the regions along the Orinoco and Apure rivers, at almost every dinner I was given venison to eat. Deer abounds in this land where there are no closed seasons and where only a limited number of hunters can shoot straight.

At Ciudad Bolívar you get some sense of the importance of the Orinoco River, which is the greatest stream in Venezuela and one of the great rivers of South America. With its tributaries, it drains 400,000 square miles and provides four thousand navigable miles. The Venezuelan government is building river boats and preparing to add to the already limited fleet in an effort to use the Orinoco to better advantage as a transportation agency.

The president discussed interestingly the power possibilities of the Caroni River which might be made accessible to the mineral as well as to the agricultural developments. As I have noted in the chapter on the Grand Savannah, this was of particular importance in the state of Bolívar, where the Grand Savannah is capable of sustaining many millions, but is now practically without population because of the transportational difficulties to the distant markets.

Ciudad Bolívar has taken on a new river activity, as material destined for the oil fields of Oficina is unloaded on the north bank of the Orinoco.

I was flown from Ciudad to Oficina in a plane accompanied by various members of the able staff of the Mene Grande Oil Company, who offered to show me the new field.

At Oficina there is emphasized again the fact that when an oil field is developed the first thought does not seem to deal with oil production. When we arrived at the camp, it wasn't the field I was shown first, but the workers' new houses which are going up at a good rate of speed. They contain all the improvements that are the result of afterthoughts that come to a man who is privileged to build a second house and to take advantage of the oversights which occurred when he built the first one. When the camp is completed for workers and staff men it will probably equal anything in Venezuela.

Someday Oficina is going to be an outstanding example of efficiency. The men there were building machine shops, warehouses, an airplane field, a small refinery for the use only of the camp; and they were laying out extensive oiled roads.

At Oficina a potential oil production of something like 25,000 barrels a day already had been developed. A pipe line was being laid from Oficina to Guanta on the sea.

All over Venezuela people are whispering about the Oficina field. It is well known that the Mene Grande had spent upwards of $30,000,000 there before it developed a commercial prospect.

At Oficina, the government is co-operating with the Mene Grande to build a road to the coast, a distance of a little over a hundred miles. This will touch an agricultural region and become a valuable addition to the growing transportational facilities of the country. A company builds the road out of its own resources, but gets credit from the government on certain port fees due the government under a legal provision which takes care of overtime in the loading of petroleum at Venezuelan docks outside of regular hours from eight in the morning until five in the evening. All shipments are made, of course, under a check-up by government inspectors, who also get overtime. Inasmuch as the oil companies have the machinery and equipment to construct roads, it has proved practicable for the government to arrange with them to build certain links in the highway system and to offset the cost of these projects by crediting the companies for the extra service which the government renders in connection with the arrival and dispatch of vessels outside of regular office hours.

# CHAPTER XXVIII

## *Automobile Traffic and the New Caracas*

---

THE PAPERS OF CARACAS are complaining about the growing nuisance of too many automobiles in the capital city. While Venezuela is still a land where 80 per cent of the population walk, nevertheless the presence of twenty thousand cars in the narrow streets of the nation's rapidly growing capital does provide a problem.

"All Caracas has become an open-air garage," yells an indignant editor. "The cars blockade the streets in daylight hours when traffic is in need of freedom. They stand out all night because there is no place in which to put them away."

The automobile traffic in Caracas in most hours of the day is fully as congested as in New York during rush periods. The handling of traffic is competent, considering the narrowness of the streets. It is a traffic in endless motion. There are few places for street park-

ing; cars circle the blocks while waiting for their passengers who are visiting the shops.

But, as I shall show later in this chapter, there are
plans to change all this in the most grandiose city-trans-
formation project contemplated anywhere in the New
World.

In the meantime, with the steadily increasing number
of motor vehicles, the driver of a car risks his personal
freedom every time he puts his hand to the wheel. Here,
when an accident occurs, he goes to jail, no matter what
the merits are, until the case has been talked over in the
traffic court. He generally spends six days in jail waiting for trial. For obstructing traffic by participating in
an accident the owner of the car gets a fine of twenty-five
bolivars. In a case of collision, owners of both cars are
fined, and the fifty bolivars paid finally by the owner of
the car declared to be responsible for the accident. If
the vehicle court declares that it was an accident in
which neither driver was to blame, the owners pay the
fine equally.

The unchangeable equation is that all owners of cars
involved in accidents pay a fine of twenty-five bolivars
for interfering with traffic.

The usual system of giving menacing tickets to those
who violate parking rules is more active here than in
any other place I've visited. It is comparatively a new
system in Caracas, and the young traffic policemen who
administer it certainly do love to be vigilant in their
duty!

One day as I sat in one of the few parking places waiting for a friend, I talked with my driver. He was a Negro from Trinidad and spoke English with a cultivated accent. He said that the regulations for driving licenses were more strict than ever before. There are now license schools which teach driving, and you cannot drive a car until you have passed the test provided under the traffic ordinances. These compel mechanistic training, and the driver must have a doctor's certificate stating that his eyes are good and his health dependable.

The law has standardized the penalties for the various things that can happen to a driver.

For killing a man by accident, a driver gets two years' imprisonment. If, after some delay while waiting in jail for trial, it is found that the accident was unavoidable, he still spends some time in jail as a sort of warning not to allow any more unavoidable accidents to occur!

My driver had just finished telling me that there were few car thefts when René Borges, for whom I had been waiting, arrived looking disturbed. He explained that he had been delayed by the theft of his car! The previous evening he had left his car in the streets, at a proper parking spot, while he went to a theater. Following a general custom, he had employed a young man to keep his eye on it until the theater was over. The youngster, who had always borne a good reputation, fell for the temptation to give himself a drive in Mr Borges' car while waiting. He met with an accident and ran away, leaving the car seriously damaged.

When I left Caracas weeks later, apparently the youngster was still running, although the car had been repaired.

One of the admirable organizations just launched by the administration for securing citizenship co-operation is called a "police school" for citizens, who were asked to study the growing problems which challenge the public safety from any angle and to give advice and active assistance in the administration of plans providing for social safety.

An unusual trait characterizes the Venezuelan leaders. They have all of the civic valor which comes from ignorance of civic dangers. They are unaffectedly eager to learn. My judgment, after spending much time with them, is that they are entirely sincere in their hope to gain new light for themselves from well-informed visitors. In pursuance of this hope they are organizing a movement to bring eminent writers, educators, students of political, civic and economic affairs, and architects to Venezuela as guests of the government, for the sole purpose of gaining from them constructive criticism and advice.

Some reflection of the optimism of the period is contained in the new plans for urbanization, not only in Caracas, but elsewhere.

The Bureau of Urbanization in Caracas is a competent-looking building, filled with studious men working over drafting boards. You wouldn't think of it as a place where they are concealing any secrets. As a matter of fact, they are getting ready to spring upon Caracas a surprise that will reverberate. The members of the planning body are devoting their entire time now to the scheme of remaking the city of Caracas. They assured me that they had not publicly discussed this plan, regarding it as yet in a premature stage, and that I was the first individual, outside the members of the committee on urbanization and the ministers, to be told of the proposed scheme.

The work is in charge of Maurice Rotival, a member of a corporation of famous French architects and city planners of Paris. Mr Rotival has many noted accomplishments to his credit, having been connected with important urbanization work in Toulon, Paris, Stamboul and many other cities.

One of his latest accomplishments was a plan for the new urbanization of Bagdad, which was accepted by the late King Feisal. Iraq, blessed by the oil revenues of the great Mosul field and feeling an artistic release of spirit, had decided to improve her ancient capital. Mr Rotival had made a plan modernizing the city, tying it up with an astonishing airport worthy to be the aerial meeting place of the oriental and occidental worlds. He was on his way to meet the king of Iraq in London for the final go-ahead orders on construction when word came that the young monarch had met his death in an automobile crash. The tragedy had caused an upset. The new Bagdad now will wait on a regency which governs for the late monarch's young son.

The new plans for Caracas are so sweeping that it is not strange the commission withholds them until they are ready to go ahead. They now approach that point.

For months, the commission and government officials have been checking, amending and rechecking the drafts until there is a room full of drawings, charts, cross sections and front elevations—all in bewildering colors that give a realistic hint of the glamour and beauty the new urbanization will bring to Venezuela's capital city.

The central feature of the downtown remodeling will be a Champs Elysées, longer and wider than the one in Paris, and calling for a street of dignified façades in the new buildings proposed for that district.

In all its past Caracas has given no thought to city planning. Nestling in a valley between mountains, it isn't possible to make a new city on hitherto unoccupied ground. Even if it were, such a move would be contrary to the philosophy both of the Paris architect and of the government commission. They do not wish to ruin the old locations but to give them added value by new civic beauty. They plan to establish new centers in old places, combining utility and grace, which will restrain the rapidly growing city from drifting too far into the canyons or up the mountainsides.

# CHAPTER XXIX

## *A Period of Relaxation*

---

I F I WERE LOOKING for an example with which to illustrate just the type of things Venezuela is accomplishing in her constructive program, I would find a basis of comparison with Mexico which, under the present Communistic movement, has done exactly what Venezuela has avoided in the past. Mexico caught from radical labor leadership the extreme leftist viewpoint and went headlong into typical Communism. Her first thought seemed to be to take away from capital, which had constructed the main props of the industrial life of the country, all that it had built, and to turn these confiscated industries over to labor and thereupon to declare that the Socialistic State had arrived.

The movement in Mexico has been entirely destructive. The workers who have been given the railroads, the oil wells, the sisal industry, the cotton industry, some of the mines and textiles have not been able to carry on effectively. Production has decreased; foreign markets, upon which Mexico's ore production depended, have fallen away until today there is an almost complete collapse not only in oil but in sisal, cotton and other commodities which engaged Mexican labor. As a result, thousands of workers are out of employment, though many of them still are on government pay rolls. Industry, grown shabby through incompetency, languishes; foreign capital upon which Mexico has depended for its major operations has sought other fields.

The Venezuelan movement is not in a political sense Socialistic. It is thinking of no new patterns. Republican in government, Venezuela has established a program to build the institutions of sanitation, education and transportation which constitute the chief needs of the Republic. When I made this investigation, the government had already spent about half of nearly a billion and a quarter bolivars which were authorized for expenditure in three years. The caution the government is exercising in its constructive work is utterly devoid of the reckless state which belongs to Communist technique.

Foreign experts are directing every technical job. There is surprisingly little graft or deliberate waste to be found in the work being done on schoolhouses, hospitals, water systems and sanitary units.

Nearly twenty new agricultural training stations, under the direction of experts who have specialized in the various values possible in Venezuelan livestock and agriculture, were already opened.

Transportation experts are carefully surveying the possibilities of added railway and highway travel. The petroleum companies themselves, through special contracts with the government, are contributing something like seven hundred kilometers of finished highways in advantageous points where they will serve both petroleum and Venezuelan agricultural regions. They are also subsidizing large hospitals for general service.

Slaughter plants for the encouragement of more productive food supply are being built by the government to meet logical needs at various strategic points in the Republic. Establishments for the processing of fish are being finished on the Orinoco River and elsewhere.

The whole picture, while somewhat elaborate, is characterized by the expenditure of larger sums of money than Venezuela could afford normally. While it may seem to the casual observer like the building of a social Utopia, it is merely the significant spectacle of a backward community's catching up through the direct aid of the State with its possibilities, probably going ahead of most of its neighbors in the enthusiasm which comes with easy spending.

But it is not teaching its labor the ways of idleness. On the other hand it is emphasizing the need of education. Its new labor law, its provisions for maintaining the balance between capital and labor, its utter freedom from political complexion has kept it a rational movement up to this moment. As a matter of fact, its program thus far has been devoted entirely to the rehabilitation of the people and follows almost exactly the line of attack laid down by the greater petroleum companies which have come here to develop their concessions.

When these effective representatives of foreign capital entered Venezuela, one of their first cares was to make safe the health of its laboring population. Thus the swamp and the jungle have blossomed with modern housings, hospitals and sanitary equipment. New emphasis upon food values and a program of clean living have taken the place of tropical sloth.

The petroleum companies have been the forerunners of high-priced sanitation and education in Venezuela.

So if today the accomplishments of the government in this direction should be a little disturbing to capital, it must not be forgotten that the idea of this same type of expenditure came not from those who stand upon a soapbox and preach the Socialistic State but from those effective capitalists who built a social program into their own industries.

The ground for concern is not that Venezuela has been taught the benefits of better food, better health and cleaner living. Human life in a land gifted with Venezuela's natural riches is fully entitled to the benefits of this character. The danger is that a spending hysteria might seize upon a people now enjoying for the first time the liberties of an open purse.

It would be unfortunate if Venezuela should lose any of that credit for good intentions and sanity which she has established throughout the capitalistic world of

Europe and the United States. While Venezuela maintained its status as a low-cost producer, its outlet into the world market grew to 500,000 barrels per day. In the last few years, as its taxes have increased the cost of production, other areas have stepped in to supply some of its rightful markets. One notable illustration is in the Persian Gulf in the Near East. Formerly, because of its higher cost, oil from Iraq could not successfully compete with oil from Venezuela. This situation now is being changed. Iraq's costs have been reduced somewhat whereas Venezuela's have been increasing constantly. A direct result is the doubling of Iraq's pipe-line facilities so that another eighty thousand barrels of oil daily can reach the market. And when it does it will displace that amount of Venezuelan oil.

Gómez visualized for this foreign capital a peculiar standardization of economy and honest expenditure. He provided a sense of security upon which a half-billion dollars of foreign investment went into the Venezuela oil fields.

Capital is skittish and full of evacuative speed. This is proven by the sad case of Mexico, which now contemplates its empty pipe lines, its sleeping oil harbor, its diminishing activities and dumbly wonders why capital has hastened away. Even Venezuela should remember that foreign capital in Latin America is always on guard against the impulses of an inflammable situation.

It built its first great reserves in Venezuela because it trusted Gómez's word of honor, which pledged an honest interpretation of the foreign contract. It believed in his careful administration which liquidated debts, built reserves and watched with intelligent keenness the manner in which capital was playing the game with Venezuela.

It ought to be within the perfect logic of the situation to maintain the status of good faith which has existed between the government of Venezuela and the foreign capital whose development of the industrial situation has made possible these large new expenditures for a social program.

The full extent of the program to which the Venezuelans have devoted themselves is not an overexpression of their present needs, but the speed with which they are driving forward may be disturbing.

Venezuela's future success in handling this new spending program depends upon the brakes which the government may be able to put upon the schedule. When its present program has been worked out within the budgetary allotments of the government, this enterprising new land should be in the mood to take a long breath and relax.

All the things that need to be cured in Venezuela cannot be treated in a glorified social program of three years—it's a job for the generations. The work of an emergency character will have been done by the close of 1941, when the Three Year Plan is scheduled to be finished. It will have placed Venezuela ahead of her neighbors, but it will also have placed her in a certain limelight which attracts the political adventurers who love a free-spending hand in government.

It also will leave her a debt which she will seek to pay promptly if she desires to maintain the credit to which the richest nation in South America is entitled. She must come to the sober realization that in her days of plenty she must plant new resources which will sustain her when she is no longer the oil Midas of the world; that diversity of sources of production and income alone can provide worth-while employment and security for her people and, through them, for their government.

It is hoped that the modern foundation she is now laying will receive, as the years go by, a superstructure built with deliberation which perfects through the slow process of the years a wall that does not shatter and scale off, a foundation that does not crumble.

All over South America there are façades that wrinkle and go to pieces in a generation because they are the work of haste and temporary vanity. The start which Venezuela has made has placed her new constructive activities upon a solid foundation. Those who know the spirit of the present leaders cherish the hope that their example will continue to guarantee the future.

# CHAPTER XXX

## The Protecting Spirit of Bolívar

---

Even in these anxious days when the European shadow touches South America with prophecy of test and trial, I expect a tranquil period for Venezuela. So far as the tragedies of the world are concerned, Venezuela has been on the side lines. Her people are not jaded by age-old nightmares proceeding out of innumerable social dislocations. They have not had to suffer from the war of nerves. Her situation is simple; she moves naturally and through logical processes to a better plane of thought and living, inspired by new social consciousness, devoid of dictatorial leadership.

This quiet country is in a safety zone, protected in a peculiar way from threat of European invasions by the neighborhood of the Panama Canal enterprise which the United States holds and guards with continuing jealousy.

Venezuela is safeguarded, moreover, by the compact

of the Western Hemisphere republics which, under the pledge of the Americas, has placed it within the circle of Pan-American protection.

There are few problems in Venezuela except those that are easily understood. The leaders are content to follow the economic and social dreams uttered by President Lopez Contreras in his first address to the Congress and reiterated on subsequent occasions.

With her economic problems largely dependent upon the richness of her mineral resources; with these resources in the hands of dependable capital from all over the world; with her people safe against want, her governmental resources firm and ample—her steady progress seems assured even in these world conditions.

There is another abiding guarantee which I believe more powerful than the tyrants. It is the force of mass thought behind the traditions of Simón Bolívar. It is difficult to explain how vitally he affects the thought of Venezuela, where he was born. Dead for more than one hundred years, his memory has become again a moving emotion inspiring thousands of young people. His statues and pictures are everywhere. He is a deity in a higher sense than the figure of Lenin has become in Russia.

Thomas Rourke, in his recent study of Bolívar, says: "His adulation is almost a cult. Half-naked Indians and ragged peons who could not decipher his name in print repeat his words as though they were spoken yesterday —whisper them in reverence and awe with a strange air of confidence that his words alone have the power to protect them from oppression."

Thus Bolívar has become in Venezuela something more than a historical personage. He is the symbol of a type of government to which they have been struggling ever since he began to teach them. So far as Venezuela is concerned, this is the heyday of Simón Bolívar's career.

It was fitting that his ghost should have walked when Gómez died. His philosophy, slumbering through the years, came to life in the land of his birth at the very time when his young countrymen of this period needed it the most. They have used it to keep Venezuela away from the trashy and tawdry materialism of the isms.

It seems altogether probable that his influence will help to give a permanence to the present republican government.

South America has never lacked pure enthusiasm and lofty patriotism, but her fluctuation into and out of dictatorship indicates a weakness for easy recourse to petty dictatorship under pressure—not as a conviction but purely as a political resort.

There isn't the slightest indication today that there will be any let-down in the spiritual determination of the new Venezuelans to keep their dreams high and their republic strong. If they retain Bolívar as their symbol and fight with proper wisdom the tropical inertia which sometimes affects the fibers of good government, they will build a Venezuela worthy to be the birthplace of Simón Bolívar.

# INDEX